What a handy and co_____ most. There's not a wasted word here. Brown has the wonderful ability to take something deep and profound and place it in a galvanizing framework. The Wisdom Circle he describes here is a simple way of grounding myself when life gets crazy. I will be returning to this treasure again and again, both within its pages and in my own mind and heart.

    MARTY SOLOMON, creator of *The BEMA Podcast* and author of *Asking Better Questions of the Bible*

I've lived most of my life in a harried state of multitasking—such is the life of a busy working mom on a mission to follow Jesus. But like many of my peers, I'm tired. I often wonder if we can truly be as effective and fruitful as Jesus envisioned his followers to be when our tanks are empty and our attention is fractured.

    Tommy's book *The Speed of Soul* is powerful because it's simple, direct, and incredibly practical. I'll be recommending it to every Christian I know.

    KAT ARMSTRONG, Bible teacher, podcast host, and author of the **Storyline Bible Studies**

Pressured by life's demands and religious ambitions, we are always racing ahead of the Spirit, striving to get more, be better, and do great things for God. Thankfully, this book doesn't shout at us to slow down. It doesn't preach peace but shares it, drawing us back gently to the unhurried rhythms of grace. There are no quick solutions here, just the quiet wisdom of someone who's learned how good it is to keep pace with the "three-mile-an-hour God."

    CHRIS E. W. GREEN, professor of public theology at Southeastern University in Lakeland, Florida, and bishop of the Diocese of St. Anthony (CEEC)

Tommy Brown's *The Speed of Soul* isn't a call to add one more practice to an already crowded schedule but an invitation to recalibrate the very shape of our lives around four simple, interlocking rhythms drawn from 1 Thessalonians 4:9-12. Having known Tommy for over twenty-five years, I can attest that this is sage wisdom from someone who isn't just writing a book but living these truths. His own steady center of gravity is a testament to the deep stillness and purpose he so generously teaches.

DR. JEREMY SIMS, professor of spiritual formation at Southeastern University

This book is for anyone who has ever found themselves overfunctioning. In a world full of hurry, Tommy's hard questions have a way of quieting the noise and drawing us back to center. He gets to the heart of the matter by digging deep into simple truths—truths that always seem to lead back to the ultimate Helper. Tommy, thank you for your relational investment in us and for courageously unpacking the stories we tell ourselves.

DEREK AND KATELYN DRYE, country duo the Dryes

Every chapter in *The Speed of Soul* flows against the cultural current to shepherd us, forward and free, into transformational inner examination. This book is a North Star guiding our hearts back home to holy reform and to the power and practicalities of Scripture as our true compass for lives of restored margin and meaning. If you're ready to step out of the frantic flow of a hectic and hurried life and into the wide-open, spacious clearing that is God's invitational rest, every page of this work is a trustworthy guide.

TANYA GODSEY, artist, speaker, spiritual director, and author of *Befriending God*

LOVE DEEPLY · LIVE QUIETLY · MIND YOUR OWN AFFAIRS · WORK WITH YOUR HANDS

Four Rhythms for a Quiet Life

THE SPEED OF SOUL

in a World of Noise

TOMMY BROWN

Published in alliance with Tyndale House Publishers

NavPress.com

The Speed of Soul: Four Rhythms for a Quiet Life in a World of Noise

Copyright © 2025 by Respokin. All rights reserved.

tommybrown.org

A NavPress resource published in alliance with Tyndale House Publishers

NavPress is a registered trademark of NavPress, The Navigators, Colorado Springs, CO. The NavPress logo is a trademark of NavPress, The Navigators, Colorado Springs, CO, registered in the United States of America. *Tyndale* is a registered trademark of Tyndale House Ministries, registered in the United States of America. Absence of ® in connection with marks of NavPress or other parties does not indicate an absence of registration of those marks.

The Team:
David Zimmerman, Publisher; Caitlyn Carlson, Senior Editor; Elizabeth Schroll, Copyeditor; Lacie Phillips, Production Assistant; Ron C. Kaufmann, Designer; Sarah Ocenasek, Proofreading Coordinator

Cover and interior image of mountains copyright © by Uyriy Kovalev/Unsplash. All rights reserved.

Author photo copyright © 2022 by Sheena Ratliff. All rights reserved.

Unless otherwise indicated, all Scripture quotations are from The ESV® Bible (The Holy Bible, English Standard Version®), copyright © 2001 by Crossway, a publishing ministry of Good News Publishers. Used by permission. All rights reserved. Scripture quotation marked KJV is taken from the *Holy Bible*, King James Version. Scripture quotations marked NIV are taken from the Holy Bible, *New International Version*,® *NIV*.® Copyright © 1973, 1978, 1984, 2011 by Biblica, Inc.® Used by permission. All rights reserved worldwide.

Published in association with The Bindery Agency, TheBinderyAgency.com

Some of the anecdotal illustrations in this book are true to life and are included with the permission of the persons involved. All other illustrations are composites of real situations, and any resemblance to people living or dead is purely coincidental.

For information about special discounts for bulk purchases, please contact Tyndale House Publishers at csresponse@tyndale.com, or call 1-855-277-9400.

ISBN 978-1-64158-631-3

Printed in the United States of America

31	30	29	28	27	26	25
7	6	5	4	3	2	1

To my children, Seri and Seth

CONTENTS

1. Finding Center: An Invitation to a Steadied Soul 1
2. (D)advice: Why We Need a Wisdom Circle 11
3. Love Deeply: How to Repair and Strengthen Relationships 23
4. Live Quietly: How to Tune Out the Noise and Tune In to God 39
5. Mind Your Own Affairs: How to Find God in the Everyday 61
6. Work with Your Hands: How to Make Meaning in Your Work 81
7. Expanding the Circle: How to Live So Outsiders Want In 111

Acknowledgments 120
Bibliography 121
Notes 127

(1)

FINDING CENTER

An Invitation to a Steadied Soul

• • • •

"Pastor Tommy, you need to find your center."

The elderly gentleman across the table from me was what I imagine when I think about a mature Christian: love, joy, peace, patience and all the rest[1] inside his cable-knit sweater-vest. I had asked him to lunch because I was floundering in my career and because he embodied the confidence, calm, and clarity that I desired. As he spoke about finding center, I wanted to nod and say that yes, yes, he was so right—but it was as obvious to him as to me that I, in my twenties at the time, had no clue what he meant.

"Listen," he went on, "the whole time we've been at lunch, you've been telling me how stressed you are. You're worried about what your coworkers think. You're running around your church trying to stamp down every problem that pops up like you're playing Whack-a-Mole. Your to-do list is longer than my arm. It's like you're standing in a field and there's a storm blowing through and you're just taking it square on the chin. You need to lower your center of gravity. You seem harried to me."

Harried—there's an odd word. You don't hear it much anymore, except from the old-timers. But it's a good word because when you say it, you feel it. And you know harried when you see it. I saw it three times this past week.

- A teenager holds her head in her hands and sobs, telling me how lonely and yet overwhelmed she feels. Meanwhile, her cell phone buzzes like a shock collar.
- A middle-aged woman receives a terminal diagnosis. Her husband stresses over how he's going to keep his job and hold together his family of four children.
- My wife and I compare calendars and realize that on Friday night our kids have three events at the same time. And we only have two children. And that's just Friday.

Harried is having more month than money, more commitments than calendar space, more stress than peace, more work than sleep, more and more and more. Always more. Harried makes you feel like if one more thing gets added to your plate, you're going to lose your mind and break the plate. Harried makes you snippy and snappy and otherwise crabby about little things that don't make a big difference.

And maybe the worst thing about harried is . . . it just happens.

Harried is the path of least resistance in a frenetic world. You know what doesn't just happen?

Calm. Content. Clear. Focused. Grounded. Strong. Spacious. Present.

In a word: centered.

Over the years, I've thought a lot about the elderly gentleman's words. Harried seemed inevitable—but centered? One doesn't just drift effortlessly into a centered life, one of internal stability and fortitude. An unharried life, I think, requires cultivating an unhurried soul.

One thing was clear: I couldn't find whatever my center was if I was taking the storm on the chin. It felt like that man knew something I didn't; something he'd learned in the school of hard knocks that everyone attends but few learn the lessons of.

As I remember his warm demeanor, I know he spoke from experience about finding his center—his presence wasn't feigned or forced; he had *become* something, had been forged into something good and beautiful and true. Like a river cutting through a canyon, wisdom coursed through this man's life, carving character into his core. And when I reflect on his graciousness and patience with me, I can't help but think that he was inviting me to yield the mountain of my hardened, resistant, striving will to the eternal flow of wisdom that had shaped his life.

I wish I'd asked him more questions during that meal. Instead, I just prattled on about another problem. I didn't know it then, but that would be our final lunch. Time passed;

we lost touch. But even though I didn't have ears to hear at the time, his words weren't lost on me. At the right moment, when the student was ready, the wisdom to find my center found me.

· · · ·

My son walked into my study as I read the Bible. He was curious and shocked to see that I had written in it, underlined sentences, colored passages—some in red, some in blue—drawn lines connecting one section to another, and doodled art in the margins. I think he was uneasy because he knows the Bible is a sacred book and marking it up must have seemed sacrilegious. I assured him that not only was this okay but also encouraged. This is a book that, yes, we read, but it is also one that we wrestle with, argue with, ask questions of. It's a book that, by its very design, offers myriad perspectives on God's mysterious ways.

The Bible is more than words on a page; it's also a canvas that invites us to color it with our experiences, to find ourselves within, between, and beyond the lines. I mark up my Bible because my Bible leaves its marks on my mind. I need space to work out what I think about it, and rather than keeping a journal handy to record notes, I imprint my impressions right there on the pages of Scripture. God's words, my words—a conversation.

Having used the same Bible for nearly twenty years, on occasion I'll encounter a note I have no memory of writing. Sometimes I'll read insights I've written that I no longer agree with. And sometimes I stumble upon a thought I long ago jotted down that arrests my heart. This was the case one morning when I read:

> Now concerning brotherly love you have no need for anyone to write to you, for you yourselves have been taught by God to love one another, for that indeed is what you are doing to all the brothers throughout Macedonia. But we urge you, brothers, to do this more and more, and to aspire to live quietly, and to mind your own affairs, and to work with your hands, as we instructed you, so that you may walk properly before outsiders and be dependent on no one.
> 1 THESSALONIANS 4:9-12

1. Love deeply.
2. Live quietly.
3. Mind your own affairs.
4. Work with your hands.

It's a simple list I forgot I'd written in the margin beside Paul's words. But more than that, it's a list that reminded me of that moment at the table with the elderly gentleman.

Although he was a Christian, the man never quoted anything from the Bible during our conversation. But this is what he was saying, or more accurately, what he embodied. It took me a decade to find language to describe what it means, as he put it, to *find your center and escape the harried life*. But here it is: As we love deeply, live quietly, mind our own affairs, and work with our hands, we create the conditions where our souls can flourish. We awaken to the life of God in us and the activity of God around us. We sink into the calm that comes from abiding in God's presence. We live from a center that holds and nourishes us. In a frenetic world filled with noise, these practices cultivate a quiet life that sustains the soul's natural rhythm—the speed of soul.

This soul-level quiet is who he was and *how* he was. This is what I hoped to become. However, at the time, I didn't have words (much less a *doable* description) to express my aspirations. But right here in my Bible's margins, though I'd had no clue what I was doing at the time, I'd left myself breadcrumbs that would lead me down a path toward steadying my soul.

My comments were written as a list in the blank spaces of my Bible. But when I read these words afresh, I saw them as though they were inside a circle. It's not that I circled them in my Bible; rather, the visual image that leapt from the page as I read the words was of them encompassed in a circle—like my mental camera was zooming in on them slowly: love deeply, live quietly, mind your own affairs, work with your hands.

So I grabbed my journal, because I needed more space than my Bible's margins allowed, and drew what I was seeing—these four phrases within a circle. Something about them being in a circle resonated with me, so I kept illustrating what I sensed about them. I suppose I could have sketched them inside a square or a triangle, rectangle, or octagon—they all have centers. But a circle seemed right.

Maybe a circle felt appropriate to me because when I think about a centered life, I see a circle: unbroken, without beginning or end, a steady boundary around a solid center. The ancients even described God as being like a circle whose center was everywhere and whose circumference was nowhere.[2]

Circles surround. Circles protect. Circles enclose within themselves what you want to focus on. Circles are elegant—smooth, curved lines in a world of jarring stops.

Circles are simple. I need simple.

Life is complex, and complexity wears me out. When I think about finding my center, I think about settling into a quiet haven—a shelter from life's harsh winds. I think about sinking from the edges of a circle to the center. I think about moving from life's extremes, where distractions and stresses abound, to the heart of things, where focus, clarity, and calm reside.

Perhaps you rarely feel centered. Challenges pummel from every direction. Something constantly demands attention. Priorities compete. Problems need solving. Work frustrates. Relationships get strained. Even good things—when too many of them tug on your immediate attention—can wear you down.

Steadying our souls requires focus: stepping back from the chaos, living from a deep well of wisdom that strengthens and guides us. Focus, perhaps, like a circle provides. A circle helps us simplify and clarify what's important. A circle creates boundaries and structure for our lives and attention.

That's why I've started calling 1 Thessalonians 4:9-12 *the Wisdom Circle*. These verses draw me in to focus on what matters most. The Wisdom Circle helps me have energy to do the things that I know God is calling me to do, to possess the resilience to be who he calls me to be, and to love the people he brings into my circle in the ways they deserve. A circle's perimeter helps guard me like a wall, keeping me close to the practices, priorities, and people in life that matter most. A circle provides a buffer from seductions that lure me back into that field where I take the winds head on, while I am opened up inside to engage the world in a healthy and centered way. It shows me an elegant, simple structure that supports spiritual vitality.[3] I think the Wisdom Circle can do the same for you.

Do you long for life-giving, stable, affirming relationships?
Love deeply.
Do you wish your life weren't so hectic and loud?
Live quietly.

Do you feel exhausted from managing your family's dysfunction and friends' complaints?

Mind your own affairs.

Do you long to make something meaningful and creative out of your life, something that makes a difference?

Work with your hands.

At our center, we all want the same things. To live the abundant life that Jesus promised. To embody wisdom like that which the elderly gentleman exuded. To feel secure and connected in our relationships. To walk with calm, contentment, and confidence. To make a difference in the world. We want what the apostle Paul offered the Thessalonian church—lives that please God and are attractive to onlookers. What more could be hoped for?

The path to that kind of life isn't easy, but it is simple.

The Wisdom Circle shows us the way.

Reflection and Discussion

• • • •

1. What does the word *harried* describe in your life?

2. Of the four things Paul prescribes—loving deeply, living quietly, minding your own affairs, and working with your hands—which one comes most naturally to you? Least naturally? Why?

3. Who in your life seems centered, as though living from a soul-level quiet place? What impact do you notice that this person has on their environment and in their relationships?

4. Why did you pick up this book? In other words, what are you seeking?

2

(D)ADVICE

Why We Need a Wisdom Circle

• • • •

"Is that your daughter?" I ask, pointing to a picture on a side table in the corner as the hygienist directs me toward the dental chair.

"Yes!" she says. "She's away at college now."

College: a topic that's been particularly front of mind for our family lately. "Do you like the college she's attending?" I ask her.

"I suppose so. She likes it, so I like it. She's in a sorority, and those friendships are important to her. And we have numerous family members and friends who live nearby and check in on her. She has a good head on her shoulders, and she's very street-smart, so we don't worry much about her."

I try to relax as the hygienist scrapes my teeth and counsels me about the merits of flossing. I've heard this speech before. I zone out and think about my own daughter, Seri, who is entering her senior year in high school. Marketing materials from universities across the nation flood our mailbox. Seri is very bright, has worked diligently, has volunteered in her community, and is boring when it comes to causing trouble—which means she has numerous options.

We've toured a handful of campuses, and in the coming year she will decide where to attend. Currently, two universities are at the top of her list. One is within driving distance; she could easily come home on weekends. The other is farther away, and we'd only see her during semester breaks. I suspect she'll attend the one farther from home. We're excited for her, though we'll be sad to see her leave.

We have a year before she'll fly the nest, and I sense that my role as her father is changing. I'm no longer the one who just gives directives. Now I'm more of a consultant. She does her thing; I give advice when asked, only intervening when necessary.

While she's in classes at her high school, I often walk into her bedroom and breathe a prayer for her: that she'll have the Lord's wisdom and favor in all that she does. Sometimes I leave a note on her pillow that says something like *Don't worry about what other people think. The truth is that most people are too busy thinking about themselves to think about anyone else.* I find myself wanting to ensure that she knows how to do very practical things that I usually do for her, like check the oil or tire pressure in her vehicle. And since I know that soon she'll have a roommate, I help her create a regimen for tidying up so the other girl won't break her neck while walking across the room in the night. I am failing, but nevertheless I persist.

I'm doing everything I can while she's in my home to ensure that she'll have what she needs in my absence. God willing, I'll be just a phone call away. And while I'll always answer those calls, my prayer is that she's equipped to handle life on her own. Our role as parents has always been to raise an adult—not a perpetual child. Now our hope is that she'll carry forward the values we instilled while she makes a home for herself in the world.

• • • •

Whether or not all of us are parents, the words we speak into the lives of the next generation carry all our hopes for their lives—that they'll learn from our mistakes and successes and be willing to hear what wisdom we've picked up along the way. That's why it's important to understand that the Wisdom Circle was meant to provide tools for the road ahead to *spiritual* children, much like I offer to my own daughter.

As far as we know, the apostle Paul wasn't married and didn't have biological children. However, he was in a very real sense a parent—someone who cared deeply about those God entrusted to him, infants and children in the faith who in turn saw him as a spiritual father. He referred to Timothy and Onesimus as his sons and thought of the members of the Christian community as his children and other family members.[1] One of Paul's favorite ways to address men and women in the early church was as *brothers and sisters*—members of a family for whom he felt responsible.[2] We can feel the pulse of his paternal heart beating through each of his letters, such as in this part of one to the Corinthian church:

> I do not write these things to make you ashamed, but to admonish you as my beloved *children*. For though you have countless guides in Christ, you do not have many *fathers*. For I became your *father* in Christ Jesus through the gospel. I urge you, then, be imitators of me. That is why I sent you Timothy, my beloved and faithful *child* in the Lord, to remind you of my ways in Christ, as I teach them everywhere in every church.
>
> 1 CORINTHIANS 4:14-17, EMPHASIS MINE

Can you sense his love? Can you hear his care when he writes, "For though you have countless guides in Christ, you do not have many fathers"? Paul wasn't in it for the money. Pastoring the church wasn't simply his nine-to-five. Like a nurturing mother, he had carried these new believers in the womb of his heart and felt the anguish of childbirth until Christ was formed in them.[3] When they suffered, he ached. When they failed, he grieved. When they succeeded, he touted their victories like a proud papa. Paul lovingly, patiently, joyfully, and often agonizingly parented the church.

As a parent, Paul wanted all those under his parental, pastoral care to thrive. However, this was no simple task. His disciples had assembled from many backgrounds and were in the slow and often aggravating process of growing in unity. Some were faithful Jews; some had worshiped foreign gods. Some were Greeks; some were so-called barbarians. Others were slaves; some were free. But in this new community that Paul had helped form, those dividing lines of hostility slowly dissolved, and they became a more diverse yet unified family.[4]

For many, this was the only family they had, because their biological relationships were strained or fractured when they chose to follow Christ.[5] And because of numerous assaults on the Christian community, ranging from harassment to martyrdom, pressure to abandon the family was severe. Paul's leadership offered a sense of much-needed security. His teaching provided a shared identity and clear direction. This family of faith desperately needed both.

· · · ·

If you were to spend any amount of time around my home, you'd hear me say the same things over and over again. "The way you do anything is the way you do everything," I tell my kids, or "Everything you do communicates something about who you are." My children call these pithy reminders *dadvice*. They know what's coming the moment I open my mouth because they've heard me tell them the same things about situations since their youth. Your parents may have done the same. I can still hear mine saying, "Shut the door! We're not air-conditioning the entire city" and still recall my grandfather's frequent reminders to "put things back where you got them from so the next time you need them you'll know where they are." To this day I make sure my tools are properly stored, oiled, and/or sharpened because, according to my father, "if you take care of your tools, they'll take care of you."

With the churches he pastored and parented, Paul was full of dadvice. And while he founded many churches in diverse locations, adapting and updating his advice to the needs and situations of each church, Paul had a core set of teachings that he repeated everywhere. Scholar J. Paul Sampley writes:

> We know from 1 Corinthians that Paul thinks of himself as having beliefs, teachings, and practices that he has [taught] in all his communities. He says as much when he describes himself as having sent Timothy to the Corinthians "to remind you of *my ways* in Christ, as *I teach them [. . .] in every church*" (1 Cor. 4:17; emphasis added).[6]

Professor James W. Thompson affirms that "references throughout the epistle to what the community already knows (2:1, 9; 3:3; 4:2, 6, 9, 11; 5:1-2) suggest that 1 Thessalonians is largely composed of repetition of the earlier [teachings] for new converts."[7] Thus, Paul's dadvice was well known and predictable. His "children" should have been able to finish his sentences.

Paul had a plan, a core curriculum, a set of teachings grounded in the ancient tradition and tailored for current events. And these teachings, this curriculum, became ingrained in the faith families he led because Paul taught

(D)advice

these same lessons, this same wisdom, over and again everywhere he went.[8]

Why was Paul so consistent in his teaching? Why did he circle back to the same well of wisdom time and again? Because, like a parent walking into his soon-to-be-adult daughter's bedroom and leaving notes for encouragement, he dispensed wisdom that would guide his children even when he was not around. His parental hopes were similar to mine. He hoped the believers would foster healthy relationships that would add value to their lives. He wanted them to remain focused on the noble things of life and not be consumed by fruitless endeavors. He desired that they'd pay attention to the gifts and callings they'd received and not waste their time conforming to culture. And he wanted to see them do meaningful work for the good of their communities rather than being lazy or, conversely, toiling without joy toward meaningless ends. He knew he needed to say it plain and clear. So when he wanted his children to know how to live, he gave them four simple instructions:

Love deeply.

Live quietly.

Mind your own affairs.

Work with your hands.

This isn't all he told them, but these four things would be enough to get them through many hardships. This small batch of wisdom would solidify the family bond. It would cultivate a culture of belonging, forging "a haven in a heartless world."[9] It would squelch squabbles and dissolve dissension. It would call for people to work together and work hard. It would form them in the image of Christ for the sake of others.[10]

As someone who had seen time's shifting sands and the world's ways, Paul was investing in the next generation the wisdom they would need to thrive. He knew how volatile were the circumstances in which they lived—political and cultural landscapes that would readily choke the life from these tender, green shoots just breaking ground. Paul tended his children carefully, drawing this Wisdom Circle around them like a trellis upon which they could grow their faith, friendships, and spiritual fruit. The Wisdom Circle became for them a sort of rule for life—a simple, clear guide to life in Christ as a family of faith.

As with any piece of wisdom, the circle doesn't say everything, but it says enough. Like any wisdom, the secret isn't in hearing but in using it. In using wisdom, you find that it applies in more ways than originally perceived. The wisdom becomes holographic in a sense[11]—as you move through life, you see it taking new shape and color as the circumstances and scenery evolve.

This is the brilliance of Paul's Wisdom Circle. He could never have envisioned the world in which we live—internet, cell phones, cyberbullying, social media, virtual meetings, travel sports, combustion engines, air travel, and on and on. But what hasn't changed much is human nature, and this is where Paul was a genius—he understood people's needs better than most. And so his advice cuts through circumstances, traversing time and space, and speaks to the heart

(D)advice

of things today. We are far removed from the cultures and climates of Paul's churches but not from their core struggles. Reading his words, or between the lines, you can see that it was as easy then as now to be a busybody (or lazy and distracted), experience relational tension, or wrestle with the meaning of work, for example. Because human nature hasn't changed, Paul's wisdom remains as relevant now as then.

This is why we need Paul's dadvice—clear, focused, doable, relevant. It's wisdom I'll tell my daughter as she prepares for college. It's wisdom I'll tell my son as he navigates middle school. In truth, it's wisdom I keep telling myself, because it's wisdom that is helping center my soul in Christ.

Paul's Wisdom Circle helps me pay more attention to my life. His wisdom calms the hurry in my soul, calls me out of the comparison trap, helps me find purpose in my work, and zips my lips when I want to gossip. His wisdom helps me become a more loving husband and father. If I can just focus here, if I can just center myself inside this Wisdom Circle—by loving deeply, living quietly, minding my own affairs, and working with my hands—while I cannot control what happens to me, I can do the work necessary to respond to life's challenges in a way that pleases God and appeals to onlookers.

But how to begin? Where do we enter the Wisdom Circle? In the same place we'll end: with love. But not just any kind of love. No, when Paul gave the first principle of the Wisdom Circle—to love more and more deeply—he had something very particular and practical in mind. Paul wrote about love with hands and feet, love that was more than sentiment and feeling. A kind of love that would strengthen relationships and deepen commitments to others. Paul wasn't thinking abstractly about love—like some nice, warm, and fuzzy feeling—but was very precise in what sort of love he wanted to see, and for good reason. He knew that our closest relationships form the heart of our existence, where wisdom will be forged or foiled.

And so it was with his spiritual family in mind that Paul picked up his pen and started to illustrate the Wisdom Circle. His first movement was deep into the heart of love, *philadelphia* love—sibling love.

A love that is largely lost in our society as we skim the surface relationally, with hundreds or thousands of connections but few truly life-giving relationships.

A love we can recover that can strengthen our hearts and bring deep joy to our days.

A love that will make brothers and sisters out of strangers and bring unity to our inner circles and congregations.

A love that leads us beyond isolation and self-interest and to the family table where everyone belongs, is beloved, and is cherished for who they are.

Reflection and Discussion

• • • •

1. What are some pieces of advice you recall from your parents or guardians growing up? How have you seen that advice bear out over the course of your life?

2. Have you experienced a metaphorical father or mother in the context of the family of God? If so, what have you learned from them?

3. Have you ever realized that Paul taught some of the same things at every church he guided? Why do you think he did this?

4. What resonates most with you from this chapter?

3

LOVE DEEPLY

How to Repair and Strengthen Relationships

• • • •

"The white tiled floors, the white walls—I just remember it being stark and sterile, white everywhere. There was nothing else in the room. No toys, no games. Just these kids they didn't know how to handle."

Debi coughs as quietly as she can to clear a catch in her throat. She apologizes for the interruption and continues the story. She does this every few minutes. I reassure her that it doesn't bother me. She's feeling well enough for a video call after the latest round of chemotherapy but not well entirely.

"They thought that these babies had demons—that they were cursed—because they were different, because of their disabilities," she continues. "And because the parents didn't want the curse to harm the rest of the family or the tribe, they either killed the babies or left them at the orphanage. Despite doing the best they could—these were good people doing important work—the orphanage staff didn't know what to do with them, so they put all of them in this white room, like somehow that would contain the curse."

"Is that where you found Sam?" I probe. "No," she responds, "but Sam's story is dramatic in other ways." Sam is Debi's adopted son. She had originally gone to Africa to adopt a baby named Joseph. But when Joseph's relatives learned that Debi is a Christian, they refused to let the adoption go through. Then came the miracle: As Debi was preparing to return home, another baby named Joseph arrived at the orphanage. She named him Samuel Joseph—Joseph for his birth name, and Samuel because of Hannah's story in the Bible in 1 Samuel. The name Samuel means "God hears."

Debi fought for Sam. No American had ever adopted a baby from his country before. Because there was no process in place, the United States embassy initially denied the adoption paperwork. Debi spent weeks working through the adoption in a war-torn region, smuggling little Samuel Joseph under a blanket from one meeting to the next because it wasn't safe for a white woman to be seen with a black baby. One night she awakened on her cot in an African hostel to discover that she was surrounded by floodwaters from a torrential rain. Then when the adoption process was completed, the airline for her return flight went on strike. Nothing was easy.

Clearly, Debi is a stubborn fighter. Here is another example of her determination: I know this is her second bout with a virtually unknown form of brain cancer and that she had survived the first after the medical team had taken extreme measures to find a remedy, at least temporarily. They told her that the cancer would return and that it would be terminal. Now here it is again.

But they don't know Debi. They don't know that, after adopting Samuel Joseph, she adopted Datch and Abby—two other babies from the same orphanage. Abby, born without bones in her knees or feet, was left alone in her crib. Five months after Debi brought her home, Abby underwent a double leg amputation.

"Her back muscles were so weak," Debi tells me. "When I'd pick her up, she was like a wet noodle. But I knew there was more going on with her." Debi smiles, rubbing the stubbled remains of her hair. "I'd leave her washcloth lying on the side of her crib, turn around, and when I'd turn back, she'd be lying there with the washcloth in her hands. We'd repeat this process like it was a game to her. She's feisty like me."

I'll never forget the first time I saw Abby, a teenager zipping around the church on her hoverboard like a New York cabbie. She looked at me with an expression that said, *You got something to say, man?* I quickly learned that sarcasm is her love language and that special treatment is not welcomed. The only help I've known her to receive is when they strapped her to the bench-press incline so she could compete in her middle school's weight-lifting competition. Nobody expected a girl who once upon a time could barely roll over in her crib to shatter the school's record. She'd go on to win multiple state titles in track and field.

"Why'd you do it, Debi?" I ask as we end our call. "You already had children. Why'd you adopt three more?"

"Because of love, Tommy," she responds, as though this is something I should already know. "Because love doesn't have to be blood. Love is a choice. Love means taking care of people even when it's difficult. Love means showing up."

She coughs and takes another sip of water. "Love is hard," she tells me, "but it's rewarding. That's what being a family is all about."

· · · ·

If you can find the center of a circle geometrically, you have a key piece of information to discover everything else you need to know about it, from radius to circumference to the other things we've forgotten from geometry. Everything about a circle revolves around its center—derives its identity, so to speak, from the center.

For Paul, the center of Christian life is love. He writes,

> If I speak in the tongues of men and of angels, but have not love, I am a noisy gong or a clanging cymbal. And if I have prophetic powers, and understand all mysteries and all knowledge, and if I have all faith, so as to remove mountains, but have not love, I am nothing. If I give away all I have, and if I deliver up my body to be burned, but have not love, I gain

nothing. . . . So now faith, hope, and love abide, these three; but the greatest of these is love.

1 CORINTHIANS 13:1-3, 13

Without love, the practice of Christian faith becomes twisted in bizarre ways for purposes other than those God intends. Without its center, Christianity becomes nothing but an ethereal concept or vague ideal, or something weaponized to gain power or control over others. On a macro scale, the universe itself would disintegrate without love, for it is held together by its Center, who is love (Colossians 1:17; 1 John 4:8, 16). So it's no surprise that at the heart of Paul's Wisdom Circle in his message to the Thessalonians is an exhortation to keep on loving more and deeper. Love is the furnace from which the fire of faith radiates; love is the bedrock of all belief. For Paul, the life of faith finds its center in love.

But how is this love expressed practically? Paul tells us in 1 Thessalonians:

> Now concerning brotherly love, you have no need for anyone to write to you, for you yourselves have been taught by God to love one another, for that indeed is what you are doing to all the brothers throughout Macedonia. But we urge you, brothers, to do this more and more.
>
> 1 THESSALONIANS 4:9-10

The Greek word here for "brotherly love" is *philadelphia*,[1] which can also be expressed as "sibling love." Before I studied this word, about all I knew about it was what some Pennsylvanians had told me—that you won't find much of it in the city of Philadelphia. For a lot of us, brotherly love may have lost much of its meaning.

But Paul knew exactly what he meant when he used this word to teach the Thessalonian church how they should live and how they should love one another. No other word could so eloquently capture his message. That's because this expression of sibling love can't help but show up in the other three elements of our Wisdom Circle.[2]

For Paul, love was not an abstract idea. When you love deeply, you will express *philadelphia* through quiet living, minding your own affairs, and working with your hands. But—and this is important—this works the other way as well. Living quietly, minding your own affairs, and working with your hands shape you into someone who *can* show sibling love to others. Like a tide that flows in and out of a bay, sibling love flows out into quiet, undistracted life and work; and quiet, undistracted life and work flow back into loving relationships.[3]

Sibling love, *philadelphia*, is the center of the Wisdom Circle. If we don't get *philadelphia* right, the shape of the Christ-formed life won't hold because we will have nothing to structure our lives around. Everything flows from the center, which means that the other three elements of the Wisdom Circle help create the encompassing radii—a way that love reaches to the margins. Sibling love is the place from which we begin to live the sort of life that pleases God and will attract outsiders (1 Thessalonians 4:1, 12).

So let's dig a little deeper into what Paul intended by his call to *philadelphia*. While this "solidarity and mutual care of siblings for each other" was a prevalent concept in Paul's day, the word itself was infrequently used in writing.[4] To understand what Paul meant when he used this word in his letter to the Thessalonians, we must consider the cultural understanding of *philadelphia* in Paul's world.

Plutarch, a Platonist philosopher and rough contemporary of Paul, lamented the lack of *philadelphia* demonstrated in his culture. As he writes in his essay "On Brotherly Love," "brotherly love is as rare in our day as brotherly hatred was among the men of old."[5] Throughout the essay's series of immensely practical instructions about how siblings should relate, a theme emerges: Brotherly love is mutual leniency displayed in "tolerance, loyalty, and forgiveness."[6]

Tolerance.

Loyalty.

Forgiveness.

Are Christians known for these three virtues? Is your church known for tolerance? It's said that most churches are known more for what they're against than what they're for.

How about loyalty? How many people in your congregation do you explicitly trust to have your back? Does gossip run amok? Do you hear people criticizing others?

What about forgiveness? Everyone in your church may agree that it is something God offers through the Cross.

But do you experience someone else's forgiveness when you wrong them? Do you offer it when they wrong you?

Now, I hope that you would affirm that your church is known for tolerance, loyalty, and forgiveness, but this may not be the norm. I suspect that love was not easy for the Thessalonian church either. Yet, as Paul writes, God is interested and invested in teaching us how to demonstrate sibling love.

Paul didn't need to elaborate on sibling love in his letter to the Thessalonians because the Holy Spirit himself instructed their hearts in the way of *philadelphia*. According to one scholar, it is entirely likely that when Paul describes the Thessalonians as "God-taught" (*theodidaktoi*), he is using a word that he invented![7] Imagine Paul searching for just the right word to express how proud he is of the church so he creates a word conveying that only God could teach this type of love. Only God could write on their hearts and minds this paramount virtue and vital lesson: that to be part of God's family means first and foremost that you show this God-taught *philadelphia*.

Understand that if Paul saw them—and us!—as siblings, he thought of them—and us!—as one family in Christ. Paul deploys sibling metaphors more than all other figures of speech—such as "body" (as in "body of Christ"), "church," and "new creation"—to describe what the disciples of Jesus should be like.[8] This is important: As far as we know, Paul was the first to ever call for sibling love from people who were not biologically related.[9] In Christ, bloodlines are not what bind us as family; rather, we are made family through allegiance to Jesus, who welcomes us into relationship with God the Father.

Paul knew that for the church to survive and thrive, God's children had to view themselves not primarily as a group or a gathering or even a body but as a family. This was more than a nice idea. For many believers, other Christians were their only family. It was common in the early days of our faith that when a person became a Christian their biological family ostracized them. Often they lost everything—inheritance and shelter in addition to familial support—when they chose to follow Jesus. In a very real and practical sense, what they needed most was not just a set of new beliefs but acceptance, support, tolerance, loyalty, and forgiveness to replace what their biological family had taken away.

This *philadelphia* has the power to make siblings out of enemies. Paul knew this well—he had earlier sought to kill the very brothers and sisters he now sought to strengthen in faith (Acts 9:1-31). *Philadelphia* celebrates diversity and erases segregation along economic, gender, and racial lines. Among families, each member is unique and brings something special to the relationships. *Philadelphia* squelches competition for status, prestige, and honor, because among siblings, your desire should be to see everyone succeed. Nijay Gupta writes:

> In Paul's world, there was a general expectation that people would compete for honor to bring glory to their own family and clan. However, within a family there existed a different mentality. . . . Family members sought to *honor* members of their own

family and defer to them. David deSilva furthermore explains that even within a family the sibling relationship "is the closest, strongest and most intimate of relationships in the ancient world." Thus, this background would all the more short-circuit any competitiveness between believers and suspicion against believers who differed in terms of ethnicity or status.[10]

What would happen if you and the Christians around you practiced this sort of deferential, Christ-centered, faith family–focused, others-minded *philadelphia*? How might it transform your life and church? Perhaps we'd find the prevailing idolatry in some churches of bigger buildings and larger attendance replaced with longer tables and smaller groups. In other words, we'd get our eyes off ourselves, our own accomplishments, our status-seeking obsessions, our preferences, and our fascinations. We'd work instead for the success of others, revel in their accomplishments, lay down our lives for their uplifting and encouragement. Maybe instead of celebrating influencers, we'd focus on supporting the weaker members of the body with tender, loving care (1 Corinthians 12:22-23). Through *philadelphia*, our bond in Christ would become our first source of identity—not our platform, politics, race, gender, financial status, clothing, or car. Church cliques would shatter because we'd foster environments of acceptance despite differences. We wouldn't let inconvenience keep us from actually meeting the practical needs of any struggling siblings. We would bear one another's burdens, rejoice with the rejoicing, mourn with the mourning (Romans 12:15).

Could sibling love inspire us to set aside our own schedules and conveniences, like my friend who used her days off to drive her elderly friend an hour each way to doctors' appointments? Could it provoke us to step outside our comfort zones, like one of my brothers in Christ who watched over a man from another church who was recovering from surgery so his wife could run some errands? Could it require personal sacrifice, like the sacrifice made by my colleague who volunteered to take a pay cut so that another colleague could receive a raise to better support his family?

Do you long for this sort of sibling affection? Sure you do. We all do. We are more isolated than ever, despite our social media connections. We are busier than ever, despite—and largely because of—the technology that promised to make our lives more efficient. We are a lonely people, gazing into the abyss of screens while real people sit next to us on the couch.

Yet we want deep friendships. We want what Scripture calls that "friend who sticks closer than a brother" (Proverbs 18:24). We want someone to have our backs. We want someone to notice us, to pay attention to us, to be a soul friend who sticks through thick and thin.

All lines in the Wisdom Circle run to and through *philadelphia*. Will we reorient our lives and reshape our mindsets to see and act as *philadelphia* leads us? Or, to put a fine point on things, will we receive and respond to what God is teaching us, as God taught the Thessalonians, about *sibling love*?

Philadelphia is costly, but it's worth it.

• • • •

When we don't understand Paul's call to sibling love, we can treat church fellowship more like a product to consume than as a family where we will be both celebrated *and* wounded. We too easily become more of the disheartened and disillusioned chanting, "I just can't connect at this church."

Despite any marketing, church is not here to offer belonging as a good to be consumed. Spiritual consumerism is an insidious disease debilitating the body of Christ. But *philadelphia* doesn't demand anything—it becomes what it hopes to receive. It welcomes whether or not it is welcomed; it affirms regardless of being itself affirmed. It shows itself a friend no matter whether anyone is friendly.

If you're feeling lonely and disconnected at church, I say this gently and with respect: Maybe it's time to look closely at how you're participating in the family. Family is where we learn to forgive, and you will need to become very good at this, because people are not perfect. Family is where we ask others how their days were instead of waiting to be asked. Family is where we show up for and celebrate each other, not making everything about ourselves. At least that's how family should be.

Yes, we ought to expect that church will be where we find fellowship. But we need to stop defining this as surface-level interaction that costs nothing and does nothing to fill our ache for relationship. Volunteers greeting people at the doors are there to help people feel welcome, but that's not the space to actually have a conversation. Sibling love requires the space and commitment for us to learn that the welcome is real—it means lots of time spent with others face-to-face.

What if every person in your church became part of your family? Not a dysfunctional, at-your-throat family—but a healthy, nourishing family? If your church is too large for that, maybe your church needs to take a serious look at its priorities, searching for ways to grow larger and smaller at the same time—reaching more people with Christ's love, welcoming them into the family of faith, and creating spaces and moments where every person can be known personally beyond being just another face in the crowd. If a sixty- to ninety-minute service absorbs the lion's share of attention and resources; if all eyes are onstage and all attention is drawn to a speaker or musician; if hardly any serious conversations can be had, few needs can be shared, milestones can rarely be celebrated, and griefs and joys can't be exchanged—then perhaps someone needs to ask, *What would it take for this church to become more like a family?*

Sibling love should be the first consideration in our church planning: All our classes and groups, services and sermons should keep Paul's ideal in mind. If what we're doing doesn't resemble Paul's prescription for a family ethos, then we need to wonder whether we've lost our way and created something that exists outside what Scripture has in mind related to *church*. We should reconsider what it would take for the church to serve its constituents and the community. We should call a family meeting and ask how we can move toward what Paul—and Christ himself—would have us do.

Philadelphia also calls us to reconsider who is in or out of the family. It leads us beyond our preferred friendships because, as theologian Reidar Aasgaard notes,

> Paul . . . describes the target group of [*philadelphia* as] "all the siblings throughout Macedonia." He does not only limit sibling language and sibling love to face-to-face relations, or to personally close relationships. . . . Paul here includes persons who lived geographically apart, many of whom were probably not personally acquainted at all. . . . Thus, Paul here presents [*philadelphia*] not as introverted, but as an open and inclusive attitude.[11]

Philadelphia isn't just about me and my local church family. It's about all Christians everywhere and reaches even beyond the family of faith to those who are not yet part of the household.

What if—whether or not you have received what you've been looking for from anyone else—you became a living, breathing embodiment of *philadelphia* inside and outside the church? What if *philadelphia* begins with you? Perhaps all you need is to ask God to teach you and then love as you're led.

Because when the whole church (as well as you and I) embodies *philadelphia*, the world will want in.

Reflection and Discussion

1. What do you think it looks like to practice *philadelphia*? Does doing so come naturally? Why or why not?

2. What about your church does and does not feel like family? What are small steps you might take to foster a greater sense of family without asking for anyone or anything else to change?

3. Who in your life best understands the reality that, more than anything else, church is a family? In other words, who do you know who gets *philadelphia* right? How does that show up in their life and relationships?

4. If your church acted like a family—showing tolerance, loyalty, and forgiveness to one another—what would change inside your church and in your community?

5. What in this chapter is most inspiring or convicting for you?

/ 4 \

LIVE QUIETLY

How to Tune Out the Noise and Tune In to God

• • • •

It's early Saturday morning as I sit at my desk typing. Outside, it's raining, gray, and mild. The house is still except for the sound of my puppy vomiting again—finally, I think, relieved of the pieces he severed from his duck chew toy. Now the mail person pulls into the drive. She struggles to open the sliding door of her van, and my older Labrador's bark pierces the silence.

Around eight, my phone buzzes—a message reminding me of a FLASH SALE at the local sporting goods store. I forgot to silence notifications; that's my fault. I also forgot to take the puppy out to use the restroom. Now there's poop on the floor. And I'm trying—for the love of God, I am trying—to find some zen state of mind to write about how in the world people like you or me are supposed to find any semblance of quiet living when the world does not cooperate.

The pace will not relent, the static will not dissipate, the dog keeps vomiting, the phone continues buzzing. Now I check Facebook for, well, whatever one checks Facebook for.

As I pour another cup of coffee, I recall a passage in Marilynne Robinson's novel *Gilead*:

> Sometimes I have loved the peacefulness of an ordinary Sunday. It is like standing in a newly planted garden after a warm rain. You can feel the silent and invisible life. All it needs from you is that you take care not to trample on it. And that was such a quiet day, rain on the roof, rain against the windows, and everyone grateful, since it seems we never do have quite enough rain.[1]

The peacefulness of an ordinary Sunday. When was the last time you experienced that?

You may want this. You might want it like I do.

But life does not want it for you and will not cooperate. Your days are busy and distracted—filled with real responsibilities that aren't done if you don't do them.

Peace, quiet, and stillness are all held hostage by daily demands.

But sometimes you stumble unexpectedly into a calm and quiet you can't articulate and didn't anticipate. Maybe it's the hypnotic cadence of rain pattering on the roof. Or perhaps the sensory delights of a freshly planted garden—the scent of fertile soil, sun kissing your shoulders, tender vegetable seedlings, black dirt beneath the whites of your nails. The quiet—that sense of serenity, centeredness, interior tranquility, oneness—is always there, hidden and liminal like a buried treasure you might trample unaware.

Some mornings you just awaken to it enveloping you when you're alone. You experience it in the middle of the day or during a stroll. You may have a moment of clarity in a noisy room full of people.

You know when it happens—that harmony between your being and Christ's presence that fills all things (Colossians 1:17)—and wish it would happen more often. Then it leaves as quickly as it came—fleeting, fading, gone.

You wish you could tune your mind to that sacred frequency and live consistently with less static, more lucidity. I know I do. It's easy for me to understand why the fourth-century monk St. Basil of Caesarea tried to persuade his friend Gregory to flee society with him in order to seek God together:

> There is a lofty mountain covered with thick woods, watered towards the north with cool and transparent streams. A plain lies beneath, enriched by the waters which are ever draining off from it; and skirted by a spontaneous profusion of trees almost thick enough to be a fence. . . . What need to tell of the exhalations from the earth, or the breezes from the river? Another might admire the multitude of flowers and singing birds. . . . However, the chief praise of the place is, that being happily disposed to

for produce of every kind, it nurtures what to me is *the sweetest produce of all, quietness.*[2]

Sounds great, doesn't it? But maybe you wonder if you've seared or severed some part of your brain that *holy* people seem to possess—the ability to be quiet.

Quiet, even for a minute.

Quiet, able to string together a sacred few undistracted, unspoiled moments.

Quiet, somehow for a whole day.

To live in the perpetual serenity of St. Basil's forest.

To endlessly dwell in the ambient warmth of an ordinary Sunday rain.

To live quietly.

• • • •

"Make it your ambition to lead a quiet life," Paul writes in our Wisdom Circle passage from 1 Thessalonians 4:11 (NIV). That's an unusual phrase, isn't it? To be ambitious about living quietly? In my early church experiences, we'd sometimes have very *energetic* revival services when the preacher would command the people at the altar to "press into" what God was doing one moment and "let go" the next. I'm always confused—am I pressing in, or am I letting go? Am I trying harder or trusting the process?

Leon Morris, who similarly wrestles with Paul's riddle, frames the paradox in two striking ways:

"Be ambitious to be unambitious."

and

"Seek strenuously to be still."[3]

Herein lies a secret to a simple life, a good life grounded in rich and fertile soil.

Among the moral teachers in Paul's time, the call to live quietly was generally a call for "living a peaceful, harmonious life, or for the inner tranquility of the individual."[4] So in encouraging his readers to be ambitious about quiet living, Paul was calling each of them to pursue a target far different from the culture's goals and aspirations: to appear different from the chaos around them, to rigorously focus on pursuing a life immersed in reflection and contemplation. A life that seasoned the culture with simple, Christ-centered compassion. A life in which every action and motive was reframed and reshaped, from their talk to their treatment of others.

In *The Philokalia*, an ancient text on Christian living, Evagrios the Solitary teaches: "Make stillness your criterion for testing the value of everything, and choose always what contributes to it."[5]

This assertion to let stillness test the value of everything can lead to some powerful personal reflection: Does this technology, purchase, or entertainment add to my soul's peace and tranquility? Does it contribute tranquility to my friends' and family's lives?

Living quietly is not some legalistic housekeeping effort where we eliminate anything that isn't explicitly Christian (only Christian music, Christian T-shirts, Christian free-range eggs, and so on). You can have a house that's full of Christian everything yet overflows with emotional and spiritual clutter. Rather, pursuing quiet requires a clear-eyed look at whether the stuff of your life contributes to the peace of your home and relationships.

Quiet living offers an antidote to exhaustion, a promise of sustainability, presence, and wholeness. When we live quietly, we live differently. We live with the volume of life dialed down, the pace of life slowed, the desires of life restrained. We show up differently to work and relationships. We foster friendships that are edifying and sustainable. We speak simple, clear, powerful words born of silence.[6] We deny senseless whims to seek the good, true, and beautiful for others as well as ourselves. We are formed into people who understand the times and know what to do because we are paying attention (see 1 Chronicles 12:32). We gain ears to hear the Spirit's whispers over incessant chatter.

Maggie Ross, an Anglican solitary, writes:

> We live in a time when we are increasingly assaulted by environmental noise and excessive information that threaten to overwhelm us. . . . If we are to adapt in the best sense of maintaining balance and integrity in the face of the onslaught of noise, we need to

learn the art of interior silence. . . . We need also to feed that silence with carefully selected information, and learn to keep at bay, to be detached from, the words, sounds, and images that create interior static, or arouse intensely negative emotions.[7]

In other words, we need to cultivate interior silence by paying attention to the external noise we allow into our lives. Quiet living cannot eliminate all the static in our lives—but it certainly reduces the static *in us*. Quiet living calls us out of a life of paying attention to everything into one in which we pay attention to what matters. Quiet living is not about withdrawal; it is about greater, clearer, calmer presence.

Paul knew that quiet living would extend beyond the Christian community. Instead of competing for status, honor, and wealth, Jesus' followers would foster sibling love among the community of faith. Because of its winsomeness, warmth, and peculiarity, that quiet living would attract the attention of outsiders (1 Thessalonians 4:11-12). A group of people ambitious about quietness, and fierce about prioritizing loving service, would certainly stand out—then as now—in an agitated, frenetic, fearful, disconnected world.

But how do we do this? How do we cultivate and curate this quiet perspective, this quiet living that is instrumental to our flourishing and health—a call that Paul compels us to seek ambitiously? To whom can we look to guide the way?

· · · ·

The *New York Times* tech journalist Kevin Roose has argued that "attention-guarding" and "digital discernment"—that is, learning to evaluate the information we're bombarded with on our screens—are essential tactics that humans will need to thrive in the age of artificial intelligence and automation. But attention-guarding and discernment were singled out as survival skills more than a millennium and a half ago, long before anyone was worried about humanity's enthrallment to algorithms and robots.[8]

We stand in a long line of strugglers seeking liberation from inward and outward noise. Since we are not the first to wrestle with quietness, we can learn from those who came before: namely, those monks called the Desert Fathers and Mothers, who withdrew to the wilderness to meet with God.

When you think of a monk, you may imagine someone living in total isolation—perhaps awakening at all hours of the night to pray, dressed in sparse brown robes, and having no fun. There's some truth in this. But we don't need to flee to the desert or withdraw to a monastery to *essentially* become monks. As fourth-century desert mystic Amma (Mother) Syncletica teaches, "it is possible to be solitary in one's mind while living in a crowd, and it is possible for one who is a solitary to live in the crowd of his own thoughts."[9] Consider also this exchange between two fifth-century monks in which quietness requires something far more fundamental than external seclusion:

One day Abba [Father] Longinus questioned Abba Lucius about three thoughts saying first, "I want to go into exile." The old man said to him, "If you cannot control your tongue, you will not be an exile anywhere. Therefore control your tongue here, and you will be an exile." Next he said to him, "I wish to fast." The old man replied, "Isaiah said, 'If you bend your neck like a rope or a bulrush that is not the fast I will accept; but rather, control your evil thoughts'" (cf. Isaiah 58). He said to him the third time, "I wish to flee from men." The old man replied, "If you have not first of all lived rightly with men, you will not be able to live rightly in solitude."[10]

Interestingly, during the medieval period, the pursuit of quiet living was probably more prevalent among people like us—people working jobs in cities, perhaps married, people living *normal* lives—than among isolated or communal monks. Professor and monastic researcher Jamie Kreiner writes, "As Piamun [the monk] pointed out, it was possible to stay single-minded without physically removing oneself from a demanding environment."[11]

Renunciation, not isolation or relationship status, made a monk. What marked the monastic spirit was rejection of the world's pace, priorities, and values rather than where the monk resided.[12]

We need not leave where we are to find the quiet life we seek. The language of *renunciation* may be beneficial for people like us who function in the hustle and flow of cities and suburbs, soccer games, school activities, and nine-to-five work life. We can be *renouncers* wherever we are and in whatever we do.

How?

Henri Nouwen reflects:

> Even when we are not called to the monastic life, or do not have the physical constitution to survive the rigors of the desert, we are still responsible for our own solitude. Precisely because our secular milieu offers us so few spiritual disciplines, we have to develop our own. We have, indeed, to fashion our own desert where we can withdraw every day, shake off our compulsions, and dwell in the gentle healing presence of our Lord.[13]

We can "fashion our own desert" wherever we are. Rather than being constrained by the various aspects of our lives—marriage, work, parenting, school, and so on—we can make these places where we focus our energies on quiet living. Our perspective can transform frustrations into invitations.

Where do we begin? Well, where did the monks begin? In all their writings, one theme surfaces repeatedly—a practice that is precisely where we should begin our search for a quiet life, for it unlocks all other progress in this pursuit. If we want to live quietly, we must begin with silence.

How much of our lives are spent talking to others and distracting ourselves simply to curtail the cacophony of voices in our heads, to avoid carefully analyzing the contents of our own interior reality?

Seventeenth-century mathematician Blaise Pascal quips:

> When I have occasionally set myself to consider the different distractions of men, the pains and perils to which they expose themselves at court or in war, whence arise so many quarrels, passions, bold and often bad ventures, etc., I have discovered that all the unhappiness of men arises from one single fact, that they cannot stay quietly in their own chamber.[14]

If Pascal were alive today, he might say that man's unhappiness arises from his inability to sit quietly even in his bathroom (know anyone who needs a cell phone to use the toilet?). Visual noise, audiological noise, mental noise, marketing, and messaging—noise all the time, everywhere. Our thoughts are rarely silent or focused, so our minds are scarcely clear. Our words do not carry the heat of spiritual fervor they might otherwise bear. Always chattering or being chattered to, we never listen to the sound of deep silence. So we speak words void of wisdom.

But, writes Ruth Haley Barton, "in the silence we become aware of inner dynamics we have been able to avoid by keeping ourselves noisy and busy."[15] It's for this reason the monks determined to vigilantly pursue silence—to slay the dragon of distraction in its lair.

The monks despised small talk because they were Olympic-grade wrestlers practicing in the gymnasium of silence to obtain the prize of interior stillness:

> Abba Theophilus, the archbishop, came to Scetis one day. The brethren who were assembled said to Abba Pambo, "Say something to the archbishop, so that he may be edified." The old man said to them, "If he is not edified by my silence, he will not be edified by my speech."[16]

Why silence? Nouwen helps us understand:

> Silence guards the inner heat of religious emotions. This inner heat is the life of the Holy Spirit within us. Thus, silence is the discipline by which the inner fire of God is tended and kept alive.[17]

Silence is the gateway to quiet living. As goes the interior, so goes the exterior—silence inside leads to quiet living in the day-to-day. Silence begins to pervade all of life, affecting everything we do and are. The work of silence is not segregated to "a separate compartment of life called 'spirituality': *it is living the ordinary through trans-figured perception.*"[18] Like the disciples who once they saw the transfigured Christ would never see him the same again (Matthew 17:1-13), silence shifts the lenses through which we see the world. It changes our perception and alters our desires.

Because of silence, we yearn to live simply. Simple, quiet living is fundamental not only to the good of the soul but also to the community's flourishing. If one person among the faith community is not living from the deep well of silence, they counteract Paul's vision for the Christian community. Such people add to the noise, distract us from what matters, lure us into trivial and frivolous pursuits, and keep us from tending the fire of spiritual heat that the furnace of silence holds for us. Simply put—they pull us out of the Wisdom Circle and into the very things we seek to leave behind. At the same time, they cause the church to miss out on what silence through that person might have otherwise produced. This is not extreme from the biblical perspective; it is the high-stakes risk and reward of taking Paul seriously in his command to pursue quiet living through the discipline of silence.

Above all—and this is what we run the greatest risk of missing—in silence, the monk hosted God's presence. This is what I long for more than anything—to know and be in communion with God. My experience is that God does not traffic in static. Like a dove who flees the sound of rustling in the bushes, the Holy Spirit seems most at home when I'm respectful of his presence and host him carefully through tender, loving attention. Silence is the space where the Spirit breathes deep in us. Isaac of Nineveh teaches:

Silence is a mystery of the age to come,
but words are instruments of this world. . . .
(K)now that every loquacious [talkative] man is
    inwardly empty,
though he discourse on amazing things . . .
If you love the truth, love silence.
This will make you illumined in God . . .
and will deliver you from the illusions of ignorance.
Silence unites you to God himself.[19]

It is a way to wholeness, the "work of silence, the re-centering of the person in the deep mind . . . where human beings share the life of God."[20]

Silence welcomes us home from the exile of our manufactured, virtual realities.[21] The intentional mind that drinks from the well of silence differs from the reactionary one sipping from shallow, contaminated streams of noise—the one that relies on wordiness for energy and is empty of any nourishment.

The fruit of silence is not just beneficial words but inherently different lives. Maggie Ross observes:

> To choose silence as the mind's default in an accelerating consumer culture—a culture that sustains itself by dehumanizing people through the unrelenting pressure of clamor, confusion, and commodification—is indeed a subversive act.[22]

Silence may be the greatest rebellion against a culture obsessed with speech, a culture where, as Nouwen states, "we hold to the deceptive opinion that our words are more important than our silence."[23] Silence exposes and disrupts this deception.

• • • •

When and how do we practice silence? Again, Nouwen points the way: "The Desert Fathers did not think of solitude as being alone, but as being alone with God. They did not think of silence as not speaking, but as listening to God."[24]

We can experience solitude—being present to God—in a crowded room. Likewise, we can experience silence—listening to God—even when we are immersed in a wordy world. Silence is a state of awareness of God with us, not solely an absence of sounds. To make this happen, we can focus on four ways of fostering silence.

First, guard your gateways—your eyes and ears. What we see and hear can disrupt the quiet in which we seek to live. St. Basil teaches the following principle:

> Do not open your ears to anyone who talks and do not respond to any chatterer during discussions that are not profitable to the goal of [discipline]. Listen to good teachings and preserve your heart by their study. Guard your ears from worldly stories lest they spoil your soul with a sprinkling of mud. Do not be interested in following the discussions of others

and nor become involved in them so as not to be manipulated nor make them slanderers. Do not be curious and do not wish to see everything, so as not to insert the poison of the passions into your thought. Only see, hear, say, and answer that which is useful.[25]

Ask yourself, *Is what I am about to hear or watch going to stir up my thoughts, cause distractions, create anxiety, or remove my mind from the present reality?* You cannot always control what you see and hear, but you can always choose to continue listening or looking. Again, this is not a moral rant about *Christian* versus *secular* (give me a secular song or film that is beautiful over a poorly written or produced Christian piece of art any day[26]) but rather an invitation to personal discernment about whether something contributes to a quiet life.

Second, guard your mouth. Approach conversations and meetings with an inclination to hear rather than to be heard. There is a time to speak and a time to remain silent (Ecclesiastes 3:7). Many of us tend first to speak rather than to listen. Instead, pause before you speak. Ask yourself whether what you are about to say will contribute to the quietness of another person's life. They may desire silence as much as you. St. John Climacus is direct in his advice on this point:

> Talkativeness is the throne of vainglory on which it loves to show itself and make a display. Talkativeness is a sign of ignorance, a door to slander, a guide to jesting, a servant of falsehood,

the ruin of compunction, a creator of despondency, a precursor of sleep, the dissipation of recollection, the abolition of watchfulness, the cooling of ardour, the darkening of prayer.[27]

Is the text message you are about to send—or the social media post you are about to share—adding to the silence? Do your words help you, and others, listen for the sounds of God in the world? The writer of Ecclesiastes teaches:

> To draw near to listen is better than to offer the sacrifice of fools, for they do not know that they are doing evil. Be not rash with your mouth, nor let your heart be hasty to utter a word before God, for God is in heaven and you are on earth. Therefore let your words be few.
> ECCLESIASTES 5:1-2

Third, guard your cell. For monks, their cell might have been a room in a secluded house or a cave in the desert. You need a place that supports your pursuit of silence where you can return on a regular basis. A former therapist told me that people should meditate in the mornings for a few minutes so that they can carry a meditative mindset with them throughout the day. When unpleasant situations arise—and they will—you will find it easier to return to a place of calm and clarity because you have practiced quietness already that day. Again, you don't need an actual monastic cell. You probably have a closet. Or a favorite chair. Or a back patio. Or a place in the woods you can sit. Abba Moses, when asked for a word of wisdom, told a brother, "Go, sit in your cell, and your cell will teach you everything."[28] When you find your "cell," and return to it regularly, then eventually *you* will become a living "cell" and carry calm with you everywhere.

Finally, guard against distraction. This was a chief adversary to the monastic mind.[29] Jamie Kreiner writes that "Christian monks saw distraction as part of a cosmic drama whose hum was especially audible in the quiet of their cells. It had become imperative to discipline distraction and stretch the mind out to God."[30] Abba Poemen went so far as to claim that "the chief of all wickednesses is the wandering of the thoughts."[31] Why? Because distraction was a form of fornication—the mind, like an errant lover, wandered from God and became unfaithful with lesser things.[32]

For Christian monks, concentration became a lifetime obsession.[33] This practice put them way ahead of their time from the perspective of neuroscience:

> [Monks like] Basil and Hildemar would not have been surprised to learn from neuroscientists and psychologists in the twenty-first century that, when it comes to nonreflexive work, the brain cannot multitask. It can only shuffle back and forth between tasks and networks, and soon enough, it starts underperforming.[34]

Of course, no one—not even monks—can fully resolve the dilemma of distraction. There are no quick fixes.[35] But we can learn from the early believers who persisted. And while no single solution solved their problem of lack of focus, they sought to focus on one thing at a time and "to identify something worthy of total concentration."[36] They were not attempting to empty their minds but to fill their minds with a thought so grand that it occupied all their mental space and expelled intruding distractions.

Here's a thought that may or may not encourage you: The monks didn't find what they were looking for—at least not for very long. But they kept trying, and sometimes succeeded. When they grasped silence—or perhaps it's better stated that silence grasped them—in fits and starts, its effects were so intoxicating and enlivening that they sought it even more despite occasional failure.

· · · ·

Silence positions us to be quiet so that we can *become* quieter. And quieter still.

We begin to seek quiet friendships with those who contribute to our silence.[37] We pray quiet prayers that focus our minds, such as the Jesus Prayer: *Lord Jesus Christ, Son of God, have mercy on me.*[38] We pursue quiet rhythms—moving and eating and resting in such a manner that our minds and bodies are clear and healthy—to aid in focus and prayer.[39] We evaluate our finances to align our purchases with things that contribute to quietness, that still our souls rather than stir us up. We seek a quiet pace, resting on the Sabbath. We make it our ambition to find quiet in all areas of life.

Until one day we begin to edify people more with our presence than with our words. Until eventually we find ourselves longing for solitude—to be alone with God—even in crowds. Until we find that the words emerging from our hearts bear the heartbeat of the Divine.

Friends, we never perfect quiet living. But in pursuing it we are made more perfect—formed into Christ's likeness for the sake of others.[40] So we give ourselves—and one another—grace. We try, and fail, and try again. That's Paul's point in 1 Thessalonians 4—it's the ambition that matters. It's the action that counts. It's the stumbling forward, it's the desiring, that strengthens us.

So let's be ambitious to be unambitious. Let's seek strenuously to be still. Let's live quietly.

Reflection and Discussion

• • • •

1. What parts of your life feel too noisy and cluttered? Where do you feel anxious and overwhelmed? What habits or routines might be contributing to the noise?

2. How might you be making the world noisier for others—in your home, friendships, workplace?

3. How can you develop an intentional habit to spend a few minutes each day in silence? When and where can you do this?

4. When you think of living a quiet life, who or what comes to mind?

5. What are some steps you can take to dial down the noise in your life?

6. Do you see Jesus as a person who lived a quiet life? Why or why not?

5

MIND YOUR OWN AFFAIRS

How to Find God in the Everyday

• • • •

How difficult is it for you to complete, undistracted and undeterred, a task that takes longer than an hour? If you work a job, how many times are you interrupted during a day, and how long does it take to regain focus? If you are retired or are a caregiver for children or the elderly, is it easy to focus on your people and chores?

Now, let's be honest: Some distraction is of our own making. How much of our time do we intentionally spend distracting ourselves from what we find too boring or daunting? You feel the urge to use the restroom. Twenty minutes later, you have caught up on your social media feed. The laundry remains unfolded; the task sits untouched. Or perhaps you're working on an assignment. You remember one of your friends recently returned from vacation. You text them to see how it went. They respond. A notification from another app pops on the screen. Now you're off the trail. You may or may not get back to the task that was right in front of you.

It's not easy to mind our own affairs. While there are many facets to this challenge, the issue tends to center on two areas: We do not mind our own affairs because (1) we enjoy meddling in other people's affairs and (2) we have never properly discerned and learned to practice the presence of God in our own daily affairs.

This is precisely what Paul had in mind when he wrote to the Thessalonians that they should mind their own affairs. This one command bears a twofold assignment, one implicit in the negative sense (what not to do) and one explicit in the positive (what to do). When we forgo the error of paying attention to what's not our business—which drains our energy and distracts us—we experience the joy and meaningfulness of minding our own business.

• • • •

When Paul writes to the disciples in Thessalonica to *mind your own affairs*, it is the only time in the entire New Testament this phrase is used.[1] But this virtue's value can be found throughout the rest of Scripture and the ancient world. Plato, who lived four centuries before Paul, taught, "To do one's own business and not to be a busybody is justice."[2] When you play your role in the community, it flourishes—this was justice for Plato. In other words, we all have something to contribute to the upkeep and flourishing of society. As Paul wrote to the Corinthian church, we are one body with many parts—each part necessary and with a distinct role to play, with no part being able to say to another part that because it is different it is unimportant (1 Corinthians 12:12-20). But when we fail to do what we can, or what we *should*, then something is missing from our common life—and we bear no small part of the blame. Playing our role while minding our own affairs is important since distraction harms not only us but the community at large.

While, so far as we know, even though Jesus never directly used the phrase *mind your own affairs*, he was clear that his followers should practice this part of the quiet life. During one occasion after Jesus' resurrection, as Peter and Jesus took a walk, Peter realized that "the beloved disciple" was following them: "When Peter saw him, he said to Jesus, 'Lord, what about this man?' Jesus said to him, 'If it is my will that he remain until I come, what is that to you? You follow me!'"[3] *What is that to you? Why does it matter what I do with him? Why does it matter if his story turns out different from yours?* Surely Jesus' response wasn't easy for Peter to accept. We do a good job of comparing ourselves to others, of minding their business because we want to ensure that we're being treated fairly.

The frustrating reality about Jesus is that he doesn't treat people how *we* think they should be treated. He treats them how *he* thinks *they need* to be treated. Take, for example, the parable of the late arrivers, where laborers who start at the beginning of the day and those who begin at the end of the day are paid the exact same amount.[4]

Henri Nouwen expresses my frustrations about this parable precisely:

> It's not fair; it's not right. If the landowner did not want to pay the full-day workers *more*, at least he could have paid them *first* and sent them away so that they wouldn't see how much the latecomers got! But no! Right in the face of those early comers who worked the whole day, the landowner pays a day's wage to the latecomers, too, thus creating an occasion for resentment.[5]

In our culture, fairness is equated with justice, and justice to our eyes is the pursuit of ensuring that everyone is treated equally. But this constant balancing of scales is not the way of Jesus. Jesus is not concerned with equal treatment. Jesus is nuanced, personalized, and attentive to each person's needs, so he doesn't treat everyone the same. To one he gives this much; to another that much.[6] To the one who has, more is given. To the one who has not, even what he has is taken away.[7] From one he calls for this sacrificial act; from another he demands something entirely different. Jesus only told one man to sell everything he owned and give it to the poor.[8] From others he gladly received the overflow of their wealth.[9]

Jesus is not fair by our standards, but you will see that he is good if you measure his judgments based on what he does with you, for you, and not for anyone else. If we believe that Jesus is over the affairs of every human being, why don't we trust what he is doing—in our lives as well as those of others?

· · · ·

These days we think we're quasi-omniscient, with endless access to the affairs of anyone and everyone. We have knowledge the first humans could never have dreamed of when they ate from the tree of the knowledge of good and evil, shooting the human project through with pain and peril.[10] Now, with a thumb's flick, we're virtually afforded near-limitless, immediate knowledge of good and evil: sex, news, sports, recipes, politics, Labrador puppies.

My friend Rabbi Arthur Kurzweil tells me that the tree of the knowledge of good and evil represents many things in the Jewish tradition but that one way to think about it is this: The tree represents knowing more than we're meant to know right now. Knowing so much information obscures our view of reality; it blocks us from knowing God.

The serpent's masterful seduction was that the tree's fruit, if eaten, would open one's eyes. At its core, the temptation was to know more, to be more—but what could be more than intimate union with the Creator? I think most of us would say now that we'd rather not know so much. Too much good, too much evil, can distract us from our real lives. Yet we still can't seem to get enough of either.

I asked Rabbi Kurzweil how he regulates the information

he consumes. He said, "I don't watch television. I don't read the newspaper. I have a few people in my life who promise to let me know if anything happens. I don't hear from them often."

"Then what do you do all day?" I asked.

He said, "I sit. I read. I think about God. Rabbi Steinsaltz says that too much useless information obfuscates our view of reality; it blocks our ability to see what's most real. You want to see reality; you don't want to live in a reality created for you by media."

He gave me an example:

> The other day I was at the doctor's office, and there was a television on the wall. In my waiting time, they told the same stories five times. There was a break-in to a home that was several cities away. Did I need to know about that? Maybe it will make me more aware. Or did I need to know about the cat that was stuck in a tree? Did I need to know about it five times? What they don't tell you is that most homes were not burglarized and most cats in my area are not in fact stuck in trees. Is the world terrible? You'd think so if you sat in my doctor's office and watched the news. That's why I want to see reality as it is, not as it's curated for me.[11]

I've thought a lot about this conversation over the years, about the tree in the Garden and burglaries and trapped cats. The longer I've thought it over, the more I'm convinced that—just as with Adam and Eve—the core of many of our problems (mine included) is that it's difficult to be satisfied with what *is*—with knowing what we know, with knowing whom we know, with being in touch with reality *as it is* and finding God in the midst of it. Poet and songwriter Andy Squyres comments:

> You don't have to know about the latest anything. You can happily be completely ignorant of all the spectacle the world is wanting you to clamor for. Go fishing. Invite the neighbors over for supper. Watch some TV. Read a poem. Pray some prayers that you know will be answered and pray some that you know won't. Be a good friend. Stay with Christ. Stay with him in your little life and enjoy it because it is such a good gift.[12]

What we choose to pay attention to determines whether we see and can receive the good gift of our little lives. Iain McGilchrist, neuroscience researcher and philosopher, notes:

> Attention changes what kind of a thing comes into being for us: in that way it changes the world. . . . [Attention] is not just another "cognitive function"—it is actually nothing less than the way in which we relate to the world. And it doesn't just dictate the kind of relationship we have with

whatever it is: it dictates what it is that we come to have a relationship with.[13]

Our attention creates our reality. What we value determines what gets our attention. Why does this matter? Because if we do not value our lives as they are, if we do not value our daily affairs—our simple chores, our routines—if we don't find our own business worth minding, we will miss out on the great gift of encountering Christ's presence in our daily moments. We will not encounter Christ by minding another's affairs—there is no invitation from Christ there, only the seductions and distractions of knowing too much.

We cannot and must not miss God in our own affairs, because when we mind our own affairs, we do what God has given us to do. Minding our own affairs, then, is properly paying attention to the gifts that God puts within our care and realm of attention. As Rabbi Adin Steinsaltz writes, "divine service in the world is divided up, with each human being, like the primordial Adam, put in charge of a certain portion of God's garden, to work it and keep it. . . . Each soul understands and does things in a way not suitable for another soul."[14]

I'm beginning to think of my small patch of land in my subdivision as my little piece of God's garden. It isn't much, but it's enough. While there is some actual gardening to do, far more extensive cultivating happens at home. Sure, there is grass to cut and there are hedges to trim—but there are also sidewalks to pressure wash, vehicles whose oil needs checking, utility bills to pay. I have children to nurture, a wife to love (and argue with, and forgive, and apologize to). There are floors to vacuum, dogs to feed and groom and pay vet bills for, air-conditioning lines to flush, toilets to wipe down, and many more things besides that that are common to all of our lives. But the ordinariness of these daily chores does not dampen their importance. Our attention should be focused on pleasing God in our little gardens of life.

• • • •

Now to the tension: Minding your own affairs cannot mean ignoring others' needs. The Gospels teach us that turning our attention away from the suffering and poor is to turn from Christ himself (Matthew 25:31-46). Christ has included the needs of others in our affairs; human pain is not a private affair—it is our business. Justin Tosi and Brandon Warmke note, "Minding your own business [can become] just an excuse for selfishly shirking your social responsibilities."[15]

Of course, even in this, balance and nuance are needed. And here is where we see how the solitude and silence of a quiet life equips us for minding our own affairs: When we live from stillness, we learn to discern between problems that are ours to solve and those that are not. Compassion—caring for and acting on the needs of others—is a limited resource.[16] You cannot possibly tackle every problem you encounter. If you think you can, you have grossly overestimated your power as well as your expertise and resources. For every person Jesus healed, he walked by others. For every mouth he fed, others hungered for bread—and he is the Son of God.

This is not to question his ability but to emphasize that the most truly human person to ever grace the earth, the most in-tune man who has lived, understood that not every person's hunger and appetite was his assignment, not every pain was his problem—*in that moment*. Saying yes to his assignment from his Father meant saying no to many other possible assignments from others along the way. But in the end he empowered others with the Spirit who empowered him and so in this way multiplied himself throughout the earth from that day forward. So, like Jesus, we must discern which needs are ours to meet and which needs are someone else's to meet.

When you do think you have the resources and insight needed to solve a problem, I suggest you should still pause to weigh how the problem may be more complex than you imagine. You may not have the expertise or ability to solve it and may end up doing more harm than good. This is a concept known as *toxic charity*[17] or, as my church history professor called it, the errant impulse to go *download some do-good on somebody*. This often isn't ministry; it's meddling. When I meddle, I think I know better than the person with the problem how it should be solved. My attempt to help is based more in my need than theirs.

It is important to help others when we can, but we cannot do this at the expense of meeting the needs that are ours to meet, that are *our* daily affairs.[18] To do this means that we will eventually end up being unable to meet anyone's needs; having failed to care for our own, we lose the ability to care for others'. Tosi and Warmke point out:

A morally good life isn't just about changing the world and shaping the revolutions of our time. Instead, it's about choosing well from among the many things that are worth doing. . . . You matter, too. If your life is so thoroughly devoted to minding others' business that you end up neglecting your own, you're letting yourself and the people close to you down. Ordinary Morality recognizes that it's not only OK to mind your own business, it's morally important.[19]

You cannot care about everything all the time. You do not need to be outraged at every injustice. You should not feel compelled to update your social media profile picture to support every cause, every problem, everything that you are told you *should* support as a morally responsible person. You will run out of energy.

There is a time to be angry, but too much leads to outrage fatigue. We can become so habituated to outrage, to being alarmed and upset, that we will not discern the moment when it's our turn to flip the tables.[20] However, it's important to remember that while Jesus overturned tables once in the presence of his enemies, he more often shared meals with countless more whom his culture had labeled *enemies*.[21] Perhaps we're too busy turning over tables when we should be setting them.

But we can, and should, do *what* we can *when* we can. Dietrich Bonhoeffer reminds us that we discern the appropriate moments and actions in partnership with God:

We must be ready to allow ourselves to be interrupted by God. God will be constantly crossing our paths and canceling our plans by sending us people with claims and petitions. We may pass them by, preoccupied with our more important tasks, as the priest passed by the man who had fallen among thieves, perhaps—reading the Bible. . . . But it is part of the discipline of humility that we must not spare our hand where it can perform a service and that we do not assume that our schedule is our own to manage, but allow it to be arranged by God.[22]

Nobody can tell you what your affairs are. Nobody can say which of the affairs of others you should seek to serve. Minding your own affairs does not in any way remove you from loving and caring for your neighbor. Rather, in focusing on your own affairs, you cultivate interior eyes to see the needs that are yours to care for—both in your life and in those around you.

• • • •

Let none of you suffer as a murderer or a thief or an evildoer or as a meddler.
1 PETER 4:15

It would be a mistake to think that the harm in minding other people's affairs is solely that it distracts us from our own. Scripture takes a much more severe view of the matter.

Peter's list in this verse strikes me as odd, as though one of these things does not belong: murderer, thief, meddler (which can also be translated "busybody"). In our culture, two of these will land you in jail. But meddling, being a busybody? Why include that in a list of such obviously dangerous actions?

Because in the life of the church, and in the life of a Christian, meddling is just as insidious a practice as the others. Professor Jeannine K. Brown writes:

> If we look at Greco-Roman conceptions of meddling, we find significant concern about and censure of such activity. In fact, we find that interfering in the concerns of others is not only frowned upon by the ancients, but it is considered by some to be subversive to the fabric of society. Thus, [*meddling*] warrants association with such terms as [*murder*] and [*theft*].[23]

Meddling may seem relatively harmless, but it is not. To put it starkly, when we meddle, we abandon our own affairs to interfere with how others pursue doing what God has assigned them to do. We undermine the structure of reality as it could be—subverting it, maligning it, conforming it to our individual will. We are playing God.

"Busybodies have boundary issues" write Tosi and Warmke.[24] They love to critique other people's *fruit*. They quote people behind their backs ("And then she said this, and then I said that, and I was like, 'Yeah, but you should . . .'"). How many of your teenager's conversations are filled with conversations about other people's affairs? How much of yours? How much do we love gossip and slander and judging the affairs of others—all while there's plenty to do in our own lives?

We think we know what should be done, imposing our morals while criticizing from a posture of supposed expertise. But, as one of the desert monks writes, "if we are on the watch to see our own faults, we shall not see those of our neighbour."[25]

Plutarch suggests that when we're focused on others' faults we become more useful to our enemies than ourselves. We're so focused on helping others improve by telling them everything they're doing wrong that we neglect our own faults. We become weaker; they become stronger.[26]

What drives us to meddle, to cross the boundary lines of our own affairs into other people's? Plutarch doesn't beat around the bush:

> Because they find their own lives disgusting, busybodies seek out others' problems and try to solve them. Rather than getting their own lives in order, busybodies root around in others' messes.[27]

Those are harsh words, but I suspect they're true. Sometimes we search out interests in others' affairs because, if we're honest, we can't bear our own lives. Perhaps I mind the affairs of others because I haven't found satisfaction in minding my own affairs. Perhaps I like letting my mind wander into other people's business because I don't have the imagination to see God in my own business. But I can—we can—see God in our own affairs.

Our meddling assumes many flattering disguises and may masquerade as a noble attempt to help others. Who isn't fond of the advocate, the activist, the helper and healer and heroine who swoops in to save the day? But beneath that generous impulse that we should or could help, is there a hint of a desire to intervene in someone's affairs because we like the *feeling* of helping? Because we get something out of it? Because we like recognition, validation, the positive feedback received from helping others? Because we even like the power of being able to control something or someone else, since perhaps our own lives feel like they lack structure and meaning?

Even if your desire to help is really about another person, have you been invited to help? Because if not, you may be "demanding their attention and pressuring them to behave as (we say) morality requires."[28]

You don't have to know what's happening in everyone's life. You don't have to solve everyone's problems. You are probably not even competent enough, and you may be more of an annoyance than you think. Better to mind your own business; when you are called upon to help another, only then can you discern whether you are competent to help. Sometimes it's best not to help but to refer the asker to someone else and then get back to minding your own business.

These days, it seems as though we've entered into an unwritten social contract to share our lives digitally in exchange for other people's attention and affirmation (or outrage) and in exchange for them sharing their lives. But minding your own affairs means keeping your affairs *your* affairs.

In an age of oversharing on social media, we may regularly keep people from their affairs by broadcasting our own affairs. How much of our lives—the wins and the losses, the pleasure and the pain—does the world really need to know? How have good, beautiful, and delightful moments in our lives been altered because we've felt the need to capture them in a photo or a video that we can share (often instantly)? Why not savor a memorable moment and linger over it longer? Why not enjoy and meditate on it? Why not hide it away and never tell anyone about it?

Social media is not the culprit—it's the *conduit*—behind a boundaryless existence. The same happens through text messaging, emails, and phone calls. Think of the interruptions in your day coming from people who pick up their phones to call or text you about things that have happened during the day. Perhaps you silence notifications and batch check your messages. But I would bet that a third to half of the items that enter my inbox are things I would never need to be made aware of. Yet I still crave knowing, so I open texts as soon as they arrive. I still send useless information to others.

Mind Your Own Affairs

According to Plutarch, this is an ancient problem:

We must, therefore, also habituate ourselves to things like these: when a letter is brought to us, not to open it quickly or in a hurry, as most people do, who go so far as to bite through the fastenings with their teeth if their hands are too slow; when a messenger arrives from somewhere or other, not to rush up, or even to rise to our feet; when a friend says, "I have something new to tell you," to say, "I should prefer that you had something useful or profitable."[29]

Just because we can share our affairs does not mean we *should*. Yes, there is goodness and beauty in being able to communicate freely with others. Sharing a silly meme can be fun. It's nice to feel connected with friends and family all over the world. I'm not suggesting you cancel your social media accounts.

But—and I am very guilty of this—just because something happens, or something comes to mind, it does not mean that I need to immediately share it. Much of what is immediately shared is unnecessarily shared. Maybe it would be better to journal about it or discuss it with a therapist; or even just ignore and forget it altogether. Perhaps I need to just think about it. Or just enjoy it. I might need time to process it. Maybe I should pray about it. Meanwhile, by not sending that text or making that call, others are freed to mind their own affairs.

• • • •

Our lives may not be all we wish. They might be filled with pain and problems and annoying people. They may, frankly, be a mess. But your life is yours to pay attention to. It is yours to care for. It is yours to make meaning of and find God in. Like Job, despite the unwise counsel of well-meaning friends, you can reject the idea that you should escape your life or succumb to hopelessness and curse God amid your wreckage, despair, and deconstruction (Job 2). Instead of these, however, seek God in your small patch of his garden—even if you're surrounded by heartache and pain. Eventually, all shall be well.

We can all grow in wisdom in minding our own affairs. Be patient with yourself. Practice paying attention to what's in front of you. Practice doing the one thing you are doing in the present moment. Practice not caring what others are up to. When you are tempted to know more than is necessary and to meddle, "shift your curiosity from things without and turn it inwards."[30] There is plenty to improve in your own life, both inside and out.

The things that are right in front of you, the people who are right in front of you day after day, they are yours to love and serve and cherish. Be responsible to your own life. Clean your house. Make your bed. Tidy your desk. Make your space hospitable. Write in your journal. Write a song. Wipe down the microwave. Organize the garage. Take a meal to an elderly friend and enjoy it with them. Host a friend and let them be themselves—entertain and enjoy rather than judging and trying to fix them. Take a walk—in the park,

Mind Your Own Affairs

through a field, on a sidewalk, or in the rain. Weed your garden. Meditate on Scripture. Set your mind on things above.

Yes, there are times to intervene in others' lives and help when needed, but most of what you are called to tend is your own affairs. And when you mind your own affairs, you create the conditions in your own soul to assist in others' affairs when warranted.

Train your mind to deal with what God is doing in your life here and now. Your life and its details are the only place God exists for you. Look for God where you are.

Reflection and Discussion

1. What do you think minding your own affairs looks like? What do you think minding the affairs of others looks like?

2. Do you mind other people's affairs more than you should? If so, why do you think this is?

3. In what ways do you neglect your own affairs in order to tend to other things? Why do you think this is?

4. How does social media shape what you pay attention to?

5. What are some areas of the little garden of your life that you want to pay more attention to?

(6)

WORK WITH YOUR HANDS

How to Make Meaning in Your Work

• • • •

A sweaty summertime rain falls on the corrugated tin roof of my father's workshop as I position one end of a ten-foot, mill-cut cypress board near the mouth of a tool called a planer. I push the wood into the planer, and the high-pitched whirring begins as a layer is stripped from the face of the board. The jagged gray surface becomes slightly smoother and less weathered, and a sense of yellowish wood tones beneath is revealed. After several passes, the board bursts with vibrant grain; it's ready to be sanded.

My grandparents and father built this workshop by hand, using mostly materials that were reclaimed from jobsites they'd worked throughout Freeport, Florida. "Dad made us back the nails out of the wood so that we could reuse them on the workshop," my father tells me.

My grandmother Mary Alice says, "We got this stretch of wood from the Aunt Becky Ward house when we tore it down."

My father and my grandmother are each missing half a finger, sliced off by the same saw that sat in the same location in the workshop for many, many years. For this reason among others, I have never once used this saw.

Vibrations from the electric palm sander tremble through my forearm. I can feel my teeth chatter when clenching my jaws. Up and down the board, always working with the grain, I run the sander until yellows and reds and greens and even hints of blue erupt from the decades-old board.

This board needs to be joined to another board that has undergone the same treatment, and together they will form the top of the long desk that my wife desires. Wrought iron table legs wait in the corner to be screwed into the underside of the tabletop. Sanding and screwing things together is the extent of my abilities, so my father joins the wood together, using tools whose names I don't know with methods he learned from his father.

My father's hands are strong and weathered, carrying scars that narrate decades of good, hard labor in the manual arts. The veins in his hands course with wisdom and intuition for making and repairing things. My hands, however, tell no such stories. Despite my father's best efforts, the contractor gene skipped a generation. I do the sort of carpentry that any child could do if given proper supervision. My mind traffics in concepts, ideas, strategies, and stories. It does not meddle in mechanics or structures and certainly not in saws.

Still, this old workshop is one of a handful of places I go when needing to rejuvenate. This space lures me, holds me, and heals me. I used to wonder if it was sheer nostalgia, or perhaps a way and an excuse to spend time with my father. But I think there's more to it than that. I'm reminded of a story my friend and teacher Dr. Chris Green heard from his friend Professor David Goa:

> David's father was quite a skilled carpenter, and he was repairing the pastor's boat. . . .
> David [is] in his father's shop as his dad is talking with the pastor and repairing this boat . . . with oak. . . .
> Eventually the pastor leaves, and David's father says . . . , "We need to pray for our pastor, because he has no oak in his life. . . . Pastors only have people in their lives, not oak. And people lie—they don't mean to, but they flatter, they exaggerate, they accuse, they beg and cajole. But you never really know whether or not the work you are doing is good when you're dealing with people. . . .
> "Tomorrow . . . I'll come down, and I will use all of my strength and I will try to break these two pieces of wood that I've glued together. And the wood and the glue will talk to me. They will let me know whether or not my work is good. And they cannot lie. They will tell me the truth. But pastors don't have that in their lives." . . .

... Do we have oak in our lives? ... That's the malaise of [our lives]. We're getting further and further from things that just tell us the truth about who we are and the quality of work we're doing.[1]

Perhaps, like me, you don't spend much time working with oak, which I'm just using as another way of saying *making things with your hands*. These days, work is less manual and more mental (a very recent historical change).[2] Andy Crouch observes that "less than 2 percent of the population in the United States in the twenty-first century are farmers, compared to 38 percent in 1900 and 58 percent in 1860."[3] Many human-centered jobs are giving way to machine-oriented jobs. Those jobs that remain human centered are increasingly ones where humans mind machines and use increasingly less creative capacity; therefore, they tend to feel less and less meaningful.[4] In no longer working with our hands, we lose touch with something of what it means to be human.

• • • •

Working with your hands—Paul's final curve around the Wisdom Circle—may seem a bit redundant, like someone saying, "Eat *with your mouth*." What else are people working with than their hands?

This was particularly true in Paul's world. He himself was a tentmaker. Most of Jesus' disciples plied trades involving bodily labor. Tradition teaches us that Jesus' mother, Mary, was a seamstress.[5] His father, Joseph, was a carpenter. Even Christ himself was a craftsman. In an age where most jobs involved making *something* with your *physical* hands, was it even necessary for Paul to identify doing so as a key part of the wise life?

Perhaps, as some scholars propose, Paul was simply telling people to get to work.[6] Maybe there was a social problem where low-status Christians were attaching themselves to benefactors, depending on handouts rather than working for themselves.[7]

It's also possible that affluent Christians looked down their noses at manual labor—after all, in the Greco-Roman world, many saw manual labor as an obstacle to leisure, a means of disfiguring the body, a hindrance to a life of wealth or fame, an impediment to intellectual activity, or one of many more roadblocks.[8] In this case, Paul would have called them down from their lofty perches into the warp and woof of the working man's way.

Other scholars suggest that early Christians were so focused on the Lord's return that they spent their days evangelizing.[9] Why should they work when Christ could return at any moment? Why work when there were so many lost souls?

But I think Paul had more in mind than dispelling laziness or overcoming stereotypes about manual labor when he used those very particular words about work—*with your hands*. I suspect he was pointing us to the creation of humanity in Genesis 1–2:

> Then God said, "Let us make man in our image,
> after our likeness. And let them have dominion over

the fish of the sea and over the birds of the heavens and over the livestock and over all the earth and over every creeping thing that creeps on the earth."

So God created man in his own image,
    in the image of God he created him;
    male and female he created them.

And God blessed them. And God said to them, "Be fruitful and multiply and fill the earth and subdue it, and have dominion over the fish of the sea and over the birds of the heavens and over every living thing that moves on the earth."
GENESIS 1:26-28

And the Lord God planted a garden in Eden, in the east, and there he put the man whom he had formed. And out of the ground the Lord God made to spring up every tree that is pleasant to the sight and good for food. The tree of life was in the midst of the garden, and the tree of the knowledge of good and evil.

    A river flowed out of Eden to water the garden, and there it divided and became four rivers. The name of the first is the Pishon. It is the one that flowed around the whole land of Havilah, where there is gold. And the gold of that land is good; bdellium and onyx stone are there. The name of the second river is the Gihon. It is the one that flowed around the whole land of Cush. And the name of the third river is the Tigris, which flows east of Assyria. And the fourth river is the Euphrates.

The LORD God took the man and put him in the garden of Eden to work it and keep it.
GENESIS 2:8-15

The beginning of our story with God begins with him working. God, being outside space and time, exists before he creates—but the first thing we are taught about God is that he works. God speaks into the deep, and light and sky, land and sea, plant and platypus spring to life. Then God creates human from humus, Adam from adamah,[10] in God's own image and likeness. There are now creatures who bear something of the divine like nothing else in creation: man and woman, God's co-laborers and co-creators in the world's ongoing care and cultivation. God made the world so that humans could make something of the world with him.

According to scholar Miroslav Volf, "one can debate the precise meaning of the *imago Dei* [image of God] in the first creation account [Genesis 1], but there is no doubt that the creation of human beings in the image of God is closely related to work. For we read that God created human beings in his image '*in order to have dominion* over the fish of the sea . . .' (Gen. 1:26)."[11] As Genesis 2 renders the Creation story, we see that "there was no man to work the ground."[12] The story ends with God sending Adam to work the very ground from which he was created.[13]

Work is a mark of what it means to be a sacred species—human beings bearing the invisible God's image in the visible world. The purpose for work—this image-bearing assignment to create and cultivate—is to *fill the earth* and *have dominion over it*.[14] *Filling the earth* is about far more than procreation—it's God's call for us to create civilization and culture, to "take this largely blank canvas he handed us on the sixth day and fill it with art and architecture, schools and services, tree forts and telescopes."[15] The other aspect of our assignment, *dominion*, is not about pillaging the earth for its resources with no thought or care for long-term consequences. Rather, the Hebrew term *radah*, from which we get the concept of taking dominion, is better rendered "loving stewardship."[16] We lovingly steward—we care for creation—as God does.

The world is off to a remarkable start. And then . . . well, you know the story. Sin. Shame. Murder. Now Adam wrestles with thorns and thistles. His work works against him, causing frustration while no longer easily yielding rewards. Eve bears children with agony. The dynamics of their relationship will change. The ground itself is cursed, along with the serpent who deceived the first couple. They are exiled from Eden, never to return.

Humans were created to work before the Fall and kept working after the Fall. But while the frustration with which they would work developed as a result of their sin, work remained inherently good. Work is not a symptom of or punishment for the Fall, because for six days God worked in creating, and we know he cannot sin. The purpose for which humans first worked remains: We were created by God, in God's image, to cultivate and create.

This may seem obvious, but we may not fully understand its importance. Perhaps, you (as I did) glossed over one small but significant detail in the Creation narrative: The river Pishon flowed "around the whole land of Havilah, where there is gold" (Genesis 2:11).

What's the point of gold in these lands around Eden? You can't eat, tame, teach, or talk with gold. When I imagine Adam and Eve, I imagine them frolicking carefreely through fields, petting fawns and blowing dandelions, planting the occasional orchard and playing in the river; I do not imagine them digging for or making things from gold.

But artist Makoto Fujimura helps us unearth a possible reason for the gold in *Art and Faith*:

> It may be that Adam and Eve were to eventually find the materials and build something outside of Eden. Build what? If there was not yet any need for them to protect themselves or shelter themselves in this time before the curses of the Fall, then what was there to build? That certainly takes imagination. But the very fact that such a passage is recorded in the Bible is a window into the mysteries of God's Creation, and of our journeys. Further, it affirms the reality of the need for imagination before the Fall—to imagine the future and create toward it. Logic will lead us to conclude that even in a sinless world, imagination, which Adam

exercised when he named the animals, existed then and exists now to forge the future—and continual creativity will be at work in the coming world. Before the Fall, we were all artists and poets.[17]

God hid gold in the ground, baking it into the crust of creation, as a contribution toward what humans would make from the earth. The first couple, or their descendants, would eventually discover and (we assume) utilize gold and other precious metals in their creativity and culture making. From the beginning, God gave us what we needed to make something with what *he'd* made.

But there's an even deeper symbolic meaning, I think, for this golden invitation to innovation buried in the hills. You see, God has a vision for the world that existed before—and that endures beyond—its fracturing by human sin. God, like a kintsugi artist, who uses gold to repair broken pottery, partners with humans and uses the metaphorical gold around us to repair the cracks, to restore what's been broken, and to continue his loving creation into the future. The ancient Jewish tradition calls this tikkun olam—the repairing of the world. Therefore, work is our sacred invitation to participate in all this repairing.

Maybe when Paul tells us to work with our hands, one reason he does so is to remind us that we come from the Creator who made us by hand—and that we, born of God's breath and formed in his image, are most truly human and most like him when we work with our hands toward creating the good, the true, and the beautiful.

We will discover that what is good and true and beautiful encompasses far more than we think.

• • • •

A pastor friend of mine reaches out with an invitation: His congregation is about to open a new sanctuary adjacent to the one they outgrew; would I be interested in a tour of the new facility before it opens?

The building is gorgeous—high ceilings, clean lines, plenty of natural lighting, tasteful aesthetic touches; they did a remarkable job. I can feel my friend's enthusiasm as he walks me through the foyer toward a back hallway. In a matter of moments, we emerge onto the stage, surveying the seats where disciples will gather for worship.

I do not expect the emotions that overwhelm me. I gush, "It's perfect. My goodness, this is just perfect. It's exactly the right size; the stage is exactly the right height. It feels like, even though there are hundreds of seats, you can personally connect with each person when you preach." I look at my friend, and he smiles with tears welling up in his eyes. I know he's dreamed of this day for many months. There's something good and beautiful about new spaces designed for the glory of God.

As is the case with most new construction, the process took longer than expected. Even as the church is quickly approaching the grand opening, parts of the work are not yet complete. My friend points at a man sweeping up some debris in the corner and explains, "He's the general contractor. He's over the entire project, and he never overlooks a detail.

If there's trash, he picks it up. And yet he's the same man who created all this." His hand gestures in the air, moving wall to wall, spanning awe-inspiring architecture.

As we take in the general contractor's work together, I find myself thinking of the Tabernacle that God commanded Moses to build long before the Temple existed. The Tabernacle was a big, tentlike structure where God met with Moses and where he was worshiped during the Israelites' desert wanderings as they moved toward entering the Promised Land. The Old Testament spares no detail in describing its construction—materials and measurements, curtains and incense concoctions, the Ark and artwork of that sacred space. That's when it hits me: why I am so fascinated by this contractor's work, why it feels so special and holy.

"Do you remember Bezalel?" I ask my friend.

"Vaguely familiar, but I don't recall exactly," he responds.

"He was what we might call the general contractor for the Tabernacle," I tell him. I open the Bible app on my phone and scroll through Exodus until I arrive at chapter 31:

> The LORD said to Moses, "See, I have called by name Bezalel the son of Uri, son of Hur, of the tribe of Judah, and I have filled him with the Spirit of God, with ability and intelligence, with knowledge and all craftsmanship, to devise artistic designs, to work in gold, silver, and bronze, in cutting stones for setting, and in carving wood, to work in every craft."
>
> EXODUS 31:1-5

Still watching the contractor, I tell my friend: "It's the first time in all Scripture that we hear that the Lord filled someone with his Spirit." In biblical studies, the *principle of firsts* means that the first time we see something in Scripture, we should pay attention to its importance.

So I consider this: A craftsman was the first person filled with God's Spirit in Scripture. Not a priest, king, judge, or any other sort of prominent figure. This suggests that *all* work—not just *religious* work, like preaching or pastoring or whatever—is sacred. God called Bezalel *by name* and filled him with his Spirit so he could make something for the Lord and his people. Perhaps this detail was included so that we would remember the sacredness of *normal* work.

"Nothing is secular—everything is sacred," teaches Charles Spurgeon.[18] British author Dorothy Sayers likewise says it plain and bold:

> In nothing has the Church so lost Her hold on reality as in Her failure to understand and respect the secular vocation. She has allowed work and religion to become separate departments, and is astonished to find that, as a result, the secular work of the world is turned to purely selfish and destructive ends, and that the greater part of the world's intelligent workers have become irreligious, or at least, uninterested in religion.
>
> But is it astonishing? How can any one remain interested in a religion which seems to have no concern with nine-tenths of his life?[19]

A lot of church preaching and discipleship focuses on admonishing those in *secular* professions to be good people outside church, attend church regularly for inspiration and worship, and give money and voluntary time to the church. *This* matters for eternity, it is thought, while the implication is that the *normal* stuff we do Monday through Friday doesn't. But, as Sayers explains, "it is the business of the Church to recognize that the secular vocation, as such, is sacred. . . . It is not right for [the Church] to acquiesce in the notion that a man's life is divided into the time he spends on his work and the time he spends in serving God. He must be able to serve God *in* his work, and the work itself must be accepted and respected as the medium of divine creation."[20]

The word *secular* can mean "without God"—which means that there is no such thing as secular work for followers of Jesus. Jordan Raynor writes, "We Christians believe that God is with us wherever we go through the power of his Holy Spirit (see 1 Corinthians 6:19). So the only thing you need to do to instantly make your secular workplace sacred is walk through the front door or log on to Zoom."[21] If we can't be holy at our work, given that we spend so much time there, there is little use trying to be holy anywhere else.

Certainly there are wicked jobs. There are ways of earning money that are anti-Christ because they are anti-human. And there are wicked people doing seemingly sacred jobs in extraordinarily evil ways—cases of misuse and abuse abound, even in churches. But most of the time, what keeps us from Paul's vision for wisdom in our work is that a lot of us are just normal people doing jobs that we can't imagine have anything to do with God.

What we need is not more people working in churches but more Christians doing good work in the world, each viewing that work as an expression of their calling. Jacques Maritain says, "If you want to produce Christian work, be a Christian, and try to make a work of beauty into which you have put your heart; do not adopt a Christian pose."[22] Or, in the apostle Paul's words, "whatever you do, work heartily, as for the Lord and not for men, knowing that from the Lord you will receive the inheritance as your reward. You are serving the Lord Christ."[23]

But even if we can intellectually assent to the idea of the sacred in all things, the reality is that we can find it difficult to see God in our work or to see our work as something that could possibly glorify God. We have wandered far from Eden, and from this vantage point, it can be challenging to see how our emails and conference calls, our cleaning and constructing—our seemingly menial, everyday jobs and tasks—can possibly bear any meaning.

But meaning, as it turns out, is what we make of it.

• • • •

Meaningless work scathes the soul. But I have come to believe that meaning (or lack thereof) does not come from one's work itself. Rather, meaning comes from what we bring to our work.

I found this lesson, in all its paradoxical beauty, in the midst of historic devastation. For months I studied the tragic accounts of Holocaust survivors. These men and women observed that in the concentration camps—a context of horrific abuse and genocide—the work's apparent meaninglessness was often the most degrading part of their experience. For instance, digging a hole only to be told to fill it back in and then having to dig it again ad nauseam demoralized a man to the point of despair. The command to carry a wet bag of salt from one end of the camp to another, set it down, and then pick it up again only to return it to the place from where it was originally—over and over—crushed the human spirit.[24]

But something surprising emerged from all my study of these captives: the refusal of some to relinquish the pursuit of meaning, even amid the terrors and drudgery of prison camp labor. Austrian psychologist and Holocaust survivor Viktor Frankl, best known for his book *Man's Search for Meaning*, writes:

> The last of the human freedoms [is] to choose one's attitude in any given set of circumstances, to choose one's own way. . . .
>
> . . . Even though conditions such as lack of sleep, insufficient food and various mental stresses may suggest that the [concentration camp] inmates were bound to react in certain ways, in the final analysis it becomes clear that the sort of person the prisoner became was the result of an inner decision, and not the result of camp influences alone. Fundamentally,

therefore, any man can, even under such circumstances, decide what shall become of him—mentally and spiritually. He may retain his human dignity even in a concentration camp.[25]

The work itself was not inherently meaningful, and there was no moral imperative upon the people in the camps to view or make it such. One would rightly forgive any person who failed to make meaning of his or her sufferings in such an environment or who failed to even try. None of this is ours to judge but only to witness. Yet, as witnesses to what Frankl and millions of others endured, we would do well to listen to what they teach us: that even in the most hideous environments, even doing the most meaningless work, we can choose to *make* meaning.

I've risked taking us into the extreme to make this single point: If meaning can be made in those circumstances, meaning can be made in ours.

You scan your badge and enter the cubicle farm five days a week. You check emails and sit through endless virtual meetings. You check social media when nobody is looking, just to get a reprieve from the monotony of your daily grind.

Or perhaps you are challenged by your job. You earn a salary that affords you time and money to do what you enjoy. But deep down, you feel like your life is meant for more, like what you're doing now does not really matter. You echo this lament from Ecclesiastes:

> Vanity of vanities, says the Preacher,
> vanity of vanities! All is vanity.
>
> ECCLESIASTES 1:2

And if you think it feels any different most days doing *spiritual* work like being a pastor, I encourage you to do some research on pastoral well-being. You may be surprised about the number of ministers who drop out of the ministry, about statistics concerning pastoral marriages that crumble and the number of pastors who commit suicide each year. Or you can just take my word for it: Religious work, by and large, is no more inherently meaningful than the *average* nine-to-five. It is what we make of it, perhaps only with stressors that other jobs do not necessarily contain.

All this begs the question *How do we make meaning of our work?* How do we—as the Preacher in Ecclesiastes determines is the best we can do—learn to *eat, drink, and find satisfaction in the work of our hands?*[26] How can we turn our work into something essentially meaningful when most days it does not feel this way?

* * *

Cutting grass is therapeutic for me—the clean, straight lines; the whir of my reel mower; dark green trimmings flipping through the morning air; the smell of the fresh cut lawn. I've worked diligently over the years to cultivate a healthy bed of Bermuda grass. But there are patches that languish because they do not receive enough sunlight. There are also, much to my chagrin, weeds—oh, the demonic torpedo grass!—creeping from my next-door neighbor's lawn into mine.

I call my friend Josh, from around the block, a man who works for a landscaping company, and ask him to look at my lawn. He comes over, stoops for a closer inspection, then stands to explain how a certain area appears to not get enough sunlight. He also shares with me how mixing a certain blend of nutrients will help. He then invites me to trim a few branches, which will help with the sunlight problem. He's very easy to understand, illustrating his points with metaphors that refer to areas of life he knows I understand better. He asks lots of good questions. At the end of our conversation, I say, "You're a good teacher. Did you ever consider becoming a professional educator?"

"I actually went to school to become a teacher," he tells me, "but then I ended up going into lawn care."

I recall a quote from Parker Palmer's book *Let Your Life Speak*: "Make me a cleric or a CEO, a poet or a politico, and teaching is what I will do. Teaching is at the heart of my vocation and will manifest itself in any role I play."[27]

To most of his clients, my friend Josh is the guy who sprays chemicals on their lawns. But today I see him clearly: He is a teacher who happens to spray chemicals on lawns. His vocation is teaching; his profession is lawn care.

We don't talk or think much about vocation these days. And when we do, we often use the words *vocation* and *job* and *profession* interchangeably. But they're not. Vocation is one's native way of being in the world. *Vocation*—which comes from the Latin *vocare,* meaning "to call"—is the way you express the essence of who you are at your core. Or, if you look back at your original human calling as God's co-creator, your *vocation* is the way in which the *voice* of God comes into the world through you—how God communicates to the world something about himself through your life.

When you understand that vocation makes work meaningful, you start to see your job—or your volunteering, caring for children at home, or retirement—as the container where you express your calling, the vessel that carries your voice. The reality of vocation is that God has a calling on each of our lives. We'd do well to get in touch with that divine calling and find meaningful ways to express it—even (perhaps especially) if our jobs are limiting. Drawing on Martin Luther, Volf says, "To be a husband, wife, child, or servant *means to be called by God* to a particular kind of activity, it means to have a vocation. When God's spiritual call through the proclamation of the gospel reaches a person in her station or profession, it transforms these into a vocation."[28]

What makes you come alive? What are you doing when you feel most yourself? Where do you see God showing up in your work, volunteering, or hobbies? When you start to see a pattern, you're on the path to understanding your vocation. By understanding your vocation, you realize that working with your hands isn't just about living your most fulfilled life. It's about making something good and beautiful of the world God created.

And so it is the same in the kitchen (a place to which I have a great natural aversion). I have accustomed myself to doing everything there for the love of God. On all occasions, with prayer, I have found [my work] easy during the fifteen years in which I have been employed here.[29]

Nicholas Herman decided to join a monastery. He wasn't a monk, however—he was simply a brother who worked in the kitchen. Eventually the book compiled from his personal writings, *The Practice of the Presence of God*, became a multinational bestseller—but he didn't create that book. Nicholas Herman, also known as Brother Lawrence, was *just a cook* who learned to practice God's presence in his kitchen.

Brother Lawrence writes that "in the noise and clatter of my kitchen, while several persons are at the same time calling for different things, I possess GOD in as great tranquility as if I were upon my knees at the blessed sacrament."[30] He decided to set his kitchen apart as a place of worship, and his kitchen ended up having the same effect on him.

Vocation is ultimately a matter of how your heart expresses worship to God in everything you do. Your work is deeply spiritual because *you* are deeply spiritual. Your work is your worship. In fact, a single Hebrew word (*abad*) can mean both "work" and "worship."[31] In this regard, there are no small tasks—there are only tiny, precious moments in the mundanity of life to give glory and honor to the Creator by how we cultivate and create in his world.

Many of us overlook opportunities to glorify God in the small areas because we are waiting to serve him in the grand and glorious parts of life. We fail to see how *this* job could be done for God's glory as we pray for him to open doors to another job where we think we can serve him better. We've been taught that we can do anything and become anything and that, if we trust him, God will do great things with our lives.

But what if I am not called to what, according to my understanding, is a great big job? What if I'm called to do work that hardly anyone notices and even fewer appreciate? What if I never amount to much of anything by societal standards? What if I never achieve the aspirations that my parents, pastors, coaches, mentors, or other influential people have spoken into my life?

Brother Lawrence would invite you to practice God's presence wherever you are. He'd invite you to see your home as a space where people can experience God's welcome, to parent your children so they know God's love through you, to see the human dignity of that person who bugs you at work, to take seriously the stewardship of your spreadsheets and logistics for God's glory.

Let's open our eyes and see right before us—among all that may be too boring, difficult, or stressful—the opportunity to do all things as for the Lord. Rather than feel trapped in our jobs, can we begin living in the freedom of trusting that God is doing far more than we know through these ordinary days? Can we choose to treat mundane and frustrating moments as chances to pay attention to God's presence?

Will we begin to see that even work is prayer if we're working mindful of the Lord? As my friend Dr. Jeremy Sims encourages, "your vocation is your pathway to be loved by God."[32] And, I would add, to love God in return.

Maybe you don't need a different job; you might just need to become a different sort of person in the job you have. Maybe you need to view doing a *good* job in your perceived *bad* job as an opportunity for God to knock the hard edges off your character and form you into the image of his Son. "The value of our activity depends almost entirely on the humility to accept ourselves as we are," writes Thomas Merton.[33] It also depends on the humility to accept our jobs as they are.

Honestly, it can be frustrating as a pastor to encounter Christians who express dreams of one day doing something great for God (like being a missionary or a worship leader, a writer or a preacher) while doing their daily work poorly and with abysmal attitudes. If we can't find God in the details of daily life, we'll surely be swallowed whole by the demands of leading in a so-called greater capacity. Character is forged, and Christ is found, in the small matters that present themselves in our ordinary jobs.

You have been endowed by God with gifts and talents that will likely be expressed through numerous jobs over the course of your life. Your work is the canvas upon which the Spirit of God paints with strokes that are unique to your hand. Your work is, or at least can be, Spirit inspired, empowered by gifts and talents that Christ has invested in you—not just for the sake of the church but also for the sake of the world, now and in eternity.[34]

• • • •

I'm uncertain when I realized that when I died I'd go to be with God forever in heaven-in-the-sky. Somehow I also believed that if I was good I'd get angel wings and a "big, big house with lots and lots a' room."[35] While the streets were made of gold, in my mind, they were also made of clouds. And I was a little concerned that I would have to sing worship songs all day.

I'm uncertain when and how all this came to be what I believed about eternity. But I'm certain not much of any of it came from Scripture. Because for all my ideas about going *up* to heaven, according to Scripture, in the end heaven comes *down* to earth: "And I saw the holy city, new Jerusalem, coming down out of heaven from God" (Revelation 21:2). God seems to have an affinity—from one end of Scripture to the other—for a divine-human partnership on the earth.

What if all along God wanted us to work and make something beautiful right now, right where we are? What if this earth is what we were truly made for? What if the goal of living well has never been to go to heaven when we die but to be truly human people made in God's image right here on this earth?

The story of humankind does not conclude with leaving the planet forevermore. It concludes with a heavenly city coming down to earth and with God dwelling with humans forever *on the renewed earth*. This is how it was in the beginning. In the end, God will continue what he began in the opening chapters of Genesis.

We now live in a middle space that some call the *now and not yet*, where Jesus is working with us by the power of the Holy Spirit *now* to build what he calls the Kingdom of God (where God's will happens unhindered) as we anticipate what is *not yet* fully here—the time when everything will be as God intends. In the *now and not yet*, we work with our hands to help bring God's beauty and goodness to the world, to help mend the fracturing due to the Fall. If we die during the *now and not yet* period, we will go to be with Christ in paradise, for "to be absent from the body [is] to be present with the Lord."[36] But in the end, our bodies will be resurrected like Christ's body was raised, and we will be part of the new city of God on earth.

If God is just going to burn the whole thing down in the end and start over, there's no point in doing anything other than praying and soul winning. (Either way, these things matter.) But if that's the case, why would Paul tell us to work with our hands? Why make art? Why play sports? Why care about the environment? Why bear children? Why tend to our homes? Because what we do now matters for eternity. The work of our hands, our co-creating with God, is part of the final destiny of creation. Jordan Raynor explains:

> After describing the New Jerusalem, John says this in Revelation 21:25-26: "On no day will its gates ever be shut, for there will be no night there. The glory and honor of the nations will be brought into [the city]."

... What is John talking about? ... Isaiah answered that question for us in the Old Testament. And even though Isaiah wrote some eight hundred years before John, scholars agree that "both men were working with the same material." So "Isaiah 60 serves as the best biblical commentary on Revelation 21–22."

In that commentary, Isaiah says this: "Your gates will always stand open . . . so that people may bring you the wealth of the nations" (verse 11). This language is nearly identical to John's. But Isaiah lists out what some of "the wealth of the nations" is.

It includes the ships of Tarshish (see verse 9), incense from the nation of Sheba (see verse 6), and refined silver and gold from some unnamed nation (see verse 9). Make no mistake about it: Ships, incense, refined silver and gold—these are all *works of human hands*. . . .

The implication here is startling. These prophetic visions suggest that some of the work of your hands—the product you're building, the book you're writing, the truck you're repairing—has the chance of literally, *physically* lasting into eternity.[37]

That final reality is why there's something primal—and I would say *God imaged*—in us saying that what we make now matters. N. T. Wright encourages us:

Every act of love, gratitude, and kindness; every work of art or music inspired by the love of God and delight in the beauty of his creation; every minute spent teaching a severely handicapped child to read or to walk; every act of care and nurture, of comfort and support, for one's fellow human beings and for that matter one's fellow nonhuman creatures; and of course every prayer, all Spirit-led teaching, every deed that spreads the gospel, builds up the church, embraces and embodies holiness rather than corruption, and makes the name of Jesus honored in the world—all of this will find its way, through the resurrecting power of God, into the new creation that God will one day make.[38]

What we do and create now matters. Even when nobody else notices, those small acts of kindness, those songs we create when nobody else is listening—the little things that hardly leave a trace—God sees and remembers those. Somehow, in the end, he will resurrect and transform those in ways that they live on with us in eternity.[39]

Our everyday work done in partnership with God matters. Like signposts pointing toward a city to which we are traveling, good work gives us a taste of the world to come.[40] Every act done in his name is a building block for those golden streets. It matters because we're made in the image of the Creator who made the first human with his hands. We are reborn by the Spirit of Jesus Christ, who is God in the flesh. He came into the world not as a politician or as a warlord but as a carpenter. He was raised by a seamstress mother and craftsman father. When God wanted to show the world what he was like and reveal the fullness of his splendor, he came as one who made things with his hands.

I don't know what you'll make. I don't know whether you're a typist, a teacher, a computer programmer, a fishing guide, or a preacher, but I know you're invited to join God in the ongoing repair of the world. So get to work. Get your hands dirty. Make something that matters to you, whether or not you get paid. In the end, it matters to God as well. Nothing is wasted.

Work with your hands.

Reflection and Discussion

1. When was the last time you worked with your hands? How was the mental, emotional, or spiritual experience of doing that different from the experience of doing other kinds of work?

2. What do you think it would look like to better practice the presence of God in your work, whatever form that takes?

3. Do you think of your work as sacred? Why or why not?

4. Why do you think God chose for Jesus to be born into the home of a seamstress and a craftsman? What does this teach us about the spirituality of manual labor?

5. What makes you come alive? What are you doing when you feel most yourself? Where do you see God showing up in your work or volunteering or hobbies, and how does this help you understand your vocation apart from a job?

7

EXPANDING THE CIRCLE

How to Live So Outsiders Want In

• • • •

Christianity has become rather noisy these days. We're clamoring for attention on social media, on television, on billboards and other ads. We want market share of the political arena and are sure to position the Christian flag near the American flag as our pundits take their pulpits and preach our political gospel of peace and prosperity. Bigger is the name of the game—congregations, budgets, buildings, worship albums. Celebrity culture is no stranger to the American church.

I suspect part of why such "Christianity" became noisy is because *we* have. I don't necessarily mean audibly loud. Rather, our lives are harried, hectic, and stressed. We are *hurried* people: reactive instead of proactive, jumping from one thing to the next, too busy to plan ahead or be intentional about *who* we want to be and *how* we want to be.

Which means we aren't living at a pace sustainable for our souls.

Which means we aren't living centered.

What would it look like if we became known for steady love and non-anxious presence? For deep and affirming and healthy relationships? For clarity and focus? For peace and centeredness? For joy and meaningfulness at work?

To get there, we have to return to the beginning of the Wisdom Circle: love. We started our journey with *philadelphia*—with Paul's command to continue practicing brotherly love for the family of faith. We express that love and create the conditions wherein it can flourish by living quietly, minding our own affairs, and working with our hands. But when we do this, the circle expands—beyond the church and into the world. Christ-centered love reaches in and reaches out.

Henri Nouwen illustrates:

> On the original cross of Jesus, we are told, the vertical and horizontal beams were of equal length. You can draw a perfect circle around the crossbeams. The horizontal beam points left toward the Jewish people, the right toward the Gentiles. The vertical beam points toward God above and to the earth below. This is the mystery and promise of the cross—the crossbeams grounded on the mountain where Jesus brings all divergent points together into one circle of God's great love.[1]

Paul says the ripple effects of living within this Wisdom Circle will reach outsiders and gain their attention. Our lives become beacons of hope:

> Now concerning brotherly love you have no need for anyone to write to you, for you yourselves have been taught by God to love one another, for that indeed is what you are doing to all the brothers throughout Macedonia. But we urge you, brothers, to do this more and more, and to aspire to live quietly, and to mind your own affairs, and to work with your hands, as we instructed you, *so that you may walk properly before outsiders* and be dependent on no one.
> 1 THESSALONIANS 4:9-12, EMPHASIS MINE

I wasn't a Christian during my childhood, so I didn't grow up thinking about my non-Christian friends any differently than about my Christian friends. Only when I became a disciple of Jesus in my senior year of high school and began attending a church did I learn about a difference between the *church* and the *world*. Before church, people were just people—some were nice; some were not. But there was not an *insider* and *outsider* mentality. Before I went to church, there was never a sense that church folk had things right and those on the outside needed their help. But attending church helped me develop a keen boundary between *us* and *them*. *They* needed *us* to come and preach to them, because without *us* they were lost.

I believe in sharing the gospel with people. I believe that apart from Christ, we are lost in a very real sense. I believe we cannot live any way we please and walk in the Kingdom of God. But I also believe there's no *us* and *them* when it comes to perceiving the benefits of the wise life. Most of my friends and family who do not attend church, the people I encounter in my daily affairs who are not Christians, have a pretty good sense of judgment about what wise and moral living looks like. That means how I live my life—the way we as God's people choose to live faithfully before him—has very real stakes when it comes to those who don't know God. Outsiders are not so bereft of sense and discernment that they don't know a good, noble, and wise life when they see one. They may not use our language to describe it, but it will resonate with them. If we live it well, they will want it badly. Paul implies this as he closes the Circle: "so that you may walk properly before outsiders," or, as other translations put it, "so that [you] may win the respect of outsiders."[2]

You can interpret this to mean that Christians should live decent, good, honest lives so that we don't lose our reputation and make Jesus look bad. Fair enough; that works. But you can also read this from the other end: that outsiders have the sense and sensibility—the discernment, if you will—to recognize good, honest, exemplary living when they see it.[3] In other words, they're not out here waiting on us to come and tell them what good living looks like with our testimonies and tracts. They will know good living when they see it because, though they may not know Jesus, they can recognize and respect a wise person who does good work. They, like us, bear the divine image. When they're close to someone who actualizes the divine-image capacity in their life, they'll know.

I'm not saying no to tracts or testimonies. Rather, I'm saying yes to living in such a way that is pleasing to God, good for you personally, and attractive to onlookers. The world longs for Christians to live in the way of Jesus—the loving, quiet, humble, hardworking way of the woodworker from Nazareth.

There's an allegorical novella by Hermann Hesse that I read every few years titled *The Journey to the East*. It tells the story of a small band of people who join "the League" and go on a great adventure. The narrator writes of one fellow traveler named Leo, who captured his attention:

> I was very fond of many of my comrades and leaders, but not one of them subsequently occupied my thoughts as much as Leo, while at that time he was apparently hardly noticed. Leo was one of our servants. . . . He helped to carry the luggage and was often assigned to the personal service of the Speaker. This unaffected man had something so pleasing, so unobtrusively winning about him that everyone loved him. He did his work gaily, usually sang or whistled as he went along, was never seen except when needed—in fact, an ideal servant.[4]

At one point in their journey, Leo disappears as a sense of impending disaster and despair permeates the League. They miss his good nature, hard work, winsome and unassuming charm, and whistling. The narrator sinks into depression, and his love for the League and the journey dwindle. He abandons the League as he searches for Leo—there is no point around which the circle of his life revolves.[5]

Eventually, the narrator reencounters Leo, and it is revealed that Leo's absence was designed as a means to test the League's loyalty to its mission. The narrator failed the test and stands before a tribunal for his sentencing. At this point, Leo's true identity is revealed—he is no mere servant but in fact the president of the League.

Leadership gurus and consultants use this tale to promote the value of servant leadership, of people in power doing small things well while serving their constituents. This is certainly a moral of the story. But the allegory strikes me in a slightly different way. When I think about Leo, I do think about servant leadership. But I'm also reminded how quiet, good living makes its mark.

I think about my middle school algebra teacher who taught with care and with a finely honed craft that made us love algebra. I think about the cart attendant with whom I worked as a teenager who took pride in cleaning golf carts, putting away members' golf clubs with care instead of throwing them into their slots (as others did). I think about the elderly man who never said much to me when I saw him at work but who wrote a check to help pay for my college education—without drawing attention to himself in the process. I think about simple people who do small things well.

My friends who don't attend church notice all the Christian noise—the sparkle and celebrity and scandal. It's difficult for them to separate Jesus from those who peddle his name. But I'm confident that's not all they notice. I'm sure they notice when Christians are excellent in their work. I'm confident they pay attention as much to what Christians don't say as to what they do say—how they don't always need to have an opinion about politics or the latest explosive topics. I think they can recognize a good husband or a good wife or children who are well trained. I'm sure they can spot a healthy home.

I know that a life of love, quiet living, minding one's own affairs, and working with one's hands is an invitational sort of life. Everyone recognizes someone with a steady soul when they cross our path.

The Wisdom Circle sits before you and welcomes you in. Sure, you will leave some things behind, but this will be a relief in the long run. The quiet and calm, the internal stillness and attentiveness of the life that Paul prescribes, is as good as it is difficult. And the difficulty is not overcome by human effort but rather by divine promise. You start where you are. You practice *philadelphia* in simple ways. As you fail, you fail forward and seek to show love better in the future. You eliminate a handful of things that add too much noise to your life; you walk in silence for a few minutes each day to clear your mind and center your heart on Jesus. You look around and notice how fortunate you are, how blessed you are, even amid the challenges. You resolve to pay more attention to your daily life and its affairs, and you seek the Spirit's guidance for where you can help others. You work with your hands—and not just with gardening and construction but also while making a puzzle with your child, while driving your elderly friend to the grocery store, while being present and engaged in your actual body with actual people. You're patient with yourself, because you understand that there's no such thing as a perfect circle drawn by human hands. No, your circle will be full of mistakes. But it's your circle. So draw it with grace and peace and enter the abundance of living at the speed of soul.

Reflection and Discussion

1. Which part of the Wisdom Circle seems like an invitation for you to grow?

2. Can you think of at least one thing you can do to implement each aspect of the Wisdom Circle into your life?

3. Why do you think a quiet life is an attractive life?

4. Think of a specific context where you have relationships with those who aren't Christians. What might change in those relationships if you started living more intentionally this way?

5. Take a few moments and ask the Lord to bring to mind some areas of your life where he wants to walk with you more closely. How can you intentionally posture yourself to experience his love and conviction in these invitations?

ACKNOWLEDGMENTS

In gratitude to David Zimmerman, Caitlyn Carlson, Elizabeth Schroll, and the rest of the team at NavPress; John D. Blase from The Bindery Agency; Austin Bailey for providing hard-to-come-by books; Dr. Chris E. W. Green for ongoing thought partnership; Alisha Brown, my mother, for typing so much of my research; and Rabbi Arthur Kurzweil for your wise and unhurried friendship. And finally, thank you to my wife, Elizabeth, for just about everything.

BIBLIOGRAPHY

Aasgaard, Reidar. *"My Beloved Brothers and Sisters!": Christian Siblingship in Paul.* T&T Clark, 2004.

Barton, Ruth Haley. *Invitation to Solitude and Silence: Experiencing God's Transforming Presence.* 2nd ed. IVP Books, 2010.

Bonhoeffer, Dietrich. *Life Together: The Classic Exploration of Christian Community.* Translated by John W. Doberstein. HarperOne, 2009.

Brown, Jeannine K. "Just a Busybody? A Look at the Greco-Roman Topos of Meddling for Defining ἀλλοτριεπίσκοπος in 1 Peter 4:15." *Journal of Biblical Literature* 125, no. 3 (2006): 549–68.

Crouch, Andy. *Culture Making: Recovering Our Creative Calling.* Expanded ed. InterVarsity Press, 2023.

Dinan, Andrew. "Manual Labor in the Life and Thought of St. Basil the Great." *Logos: A Journal of Catholic Thought and Culture* 12, no. 4 (2009): 133–57.

Frankl, Viktor E. *Man's Search for Meaning*. Beacon Press, 2006.

Fujimura, Makoto. *Art and Faith: A Theology of Making*. Yale University Press, 2020.

Green, Chris E. W., host. *Speakeasy Theology*. Podcast. "Falling into the Mind of Christ: A Conversation with Martin Shaw." June 12, 2024. https://cewgreen.substack.com/p/falling-into-the-mind-of-Christ.

Gupta, Nijay K. *1 and 2 Thessalonians*. Zondervan Critical Introductions to the New Testament. Zondervan Academic, 2019.

Hesse, Hermann. *The Journey to the East*. Translated by Hilda Rosner. Martino, 2011.

Hester, David. *The Jesus Prayer: A Gift from the Fathers*. Conciliar Press, 2001.

Holmes, Augustine. *A Life Pleasing to God: The Spirituality of the Rules of St Basil*. Cistercian, 2000.

John Paul II. *Laborem Exercens* [On Human Work]. Encyclical letter. The Holy See, September 14, 1981. https://www.vatican.va/content/john-paul-ii/en/encyclicals/documents/hf_jp-ii_enc_14091981_laborem-exercens.pdf.

Johnston, William, ed. *The Cloud of Unknowing and the Book of Privy Counseling*. Image Books, 2005.

Bibliography

Jung, Joanne, and Rick Langer. "The Strange Tale of How Nicholas Herman Found Meaning in Life." *The Good Book Blog*. Biola University, October 31, 2022. https://www.biola.edu/blogs/good-book-blog/2022/the-strange-tale-of-how-nicholas-herman-found-meaning-in-life.

Kreiner, Jamie. *The Wandering Mind: What Medieval Monks Tell Us about Distraction*. Liveright, 2023.

Lawrence, Brother. *The Practice of the Presence of God*. Translated by John J. Delaney. Image Books, 1977.

Lupton, Robert D. *Toxic Charity: How Churches and Charities Hurt Those They Help (and How to Reverse It)*. HarperOne, 2012.

McGilchrist, Iain. *Ways of Attending: How Our Divided Brain Constructs the World*. Routledge, 2018.

Merton, Thomas, trans. *The Wisdom of the Desert: Sayings from the Desert Fathers of the Fourth Century*. New Directions, 1970.

Morris, Leon. *The First and Second Epistles to the Thessalonians*. Rev. ed. The New International Commentary on the New Testament. Eerdmans, 1991.

Mulholland, M. Robert Jr. *Invitation to a Journey: A Road Map for Spiritual Formation*. Expanded by Ruth Haley Barton. IVP Books, 2016.

Nadolny, Sten. *The Discovery of Slowness*. Translated by Ralph Freedman. Paul Dry Books, 2005.

Nouwen, Henri J. M. *The Way of the Heart*. Ballantine Books, 1983.

Nouwen, Henri J. M., with Michael J. Christensen and Rebecca J. Laird. *Spiritual Formation: Following the Movements of the Spirit*. HarperOne, 2010.

Nouwen, Henri J. M., with Michael J. Christensen and Rebecca J. Laird. *Spiritual Direction: Wisdom for the Long Walk of Faith*. HarperOne, 2006.

Palmer, Parker J. *Let Your Life Speak: Listening for the Voice of Vocation*. Jossey-Bass, 2000.

Pascal, Blaise. *Pascal's Pensées*. Translated by W. F. Trotter. E. P. Dutton, 1958.

Peterson, Jordan B., host. *The Jordan B. Peterson Podcast*. Episode 472, "A Call to the Sane—Beauty, Truth, & Purpose with Douglas Murray." August 7, 2024. YouTube, August 15, 2024. https://www.youtube.com/watch?v=Rx68_EfSJsE.

Plutarch. *Moralia*. Translated by William Clark Helmbold. Loeb Classical Library 337. Vol. 6. Harvard University Press, 1939.

Raynor, Jordan. *The Sacredness of Secular Work: 4 Ways Your Job Matters for Eternity (Even When You're Not Sharing the Gospel)*. Waterbrook, 2024.

Robinson, Marilynne. *Gilead*. Macmillan, 2005.

Bibliography

Roose, Kevin. *Futureproof: 9 Rules for Humans in the Age of Automation*. Random House, 2021.

Ross, Maggie. *Silence: A User's Guide*. 2 vols. Cascade Books, 2014, 2018.

Sampley, J. Paul. *Walking in Love: Moral Progress and Spiritual Growth with the Apostle Paul*. Fortress Press, 2016.

Sayers, Dorothy L. "Why Work?" In *Letters to a Diminished Church: Passionate Arguments for the Relevance of Christian Doctrine*, 125–46. W Publishing Group, 2004.

Smith, Russell. "YOLO: A Meditation on Ecclesiastes 2:1-11 (Part 2)." *Horizons of the Possible* (blog), August 19, 2013. https://russellbsmith.com/2013/08/19/yolo-a-meditation-on-ecclesiastes-21-11-part-2.

St. Basil the Great. *The Monastic Rule of St Basil the Great*. Translated by Anna Skoubourdis and Monaxi Agapi. Virgin Mary of Australia and Oceania, 2020.

St. John of the Ladder. *The Ladder of Divine Ascent*. Translated by Archimandrite Lazarus Moore. Independently published, 2019.

St. Nikodimos of the Holy Mountain, and St. Makarios of Corinth, comps. *The Philokalia: The Complete Text*. Vol. 1. Translated and edited by G. E. H. Palmer, Philip Sherrard, and Kallistos Ware. Faber and Faber, 1983.

Steinsaltz, Adin. *The Thirteen Petalled Rose: A Discourse on the Essence of Jewish Existence and Belief.* Rev. ed. Translated by Yehuda Hanegbi. Maggid Books, 2010.

Theophrastus. *The Characters of Theophrastus.* Frederic S. Hill, 1831. https://classicalliberalarts.com/resources/THEOPHRASTUS_CHARACTERS.pdf.

Thompson, James W. *Moral Formation according to Paul: The Context and Coherence of Pauline Ethics.* Baker Academic, 2011.

Tosi, Justin, and Brandon Warmke. *Why It's OK to Mind Your Own Business.* Routledge, 2023.

Volf, Miroslav. *Work in the Spirit: Toward a Theology of Work.* Wipf and Stock, 2001.

Ward, Benedicta, trans. *The Sayings of the Desert Fathers: The Alphabetical Collection.* Rev. ed. Cistercian, 1984.

Wiesel, Elie. *Night.* Translated by Marion Wiesel. Hill and Wang, 2006.

Williams, Rowan. *The Way of St Benedict.* Bloomsbury Continuum, 2020.

Wright, N. T. *Surprised by Hope: Rethinking Heaven, the Resurrection, and the Mission of the Church.* HarperOne, 2008.

NOTES

1 | FINDING CENTER
1. Galatians 5:22-23.
2. Maggie Ross writes, "'God is a circle whose centre is everywhere and whose circumference is nowhere' is an aphorism whose origins can be traced back as far as the pre-Socratics, although this particular formulation does not appear until the third century AD in the *Corpus Hermeticum*." Maggie Ross, *Silence: A User's Guide*, vol. 1, *Process* (Cascade Books, 2014), 92.
3. Based on the concept of "boundary maintenance" as a source of group ethos and identity from Miroslav Volf, "Christliche Identität und Differenz," cited in James W. Thompson, *Moral Formation according to Paul: The Context and Coherence of Pauline Ethics* (Baker Academic, 2011), 19.

2 | (D)ADVICE
1. *Referred to Timothy and Onesimus as his sons*: 1 Timothy 1:2, NIV; Philemon 1:10, NIV. *Thought of the Christian community as his children*: e.g., 2 Corinthians 12:14-15; 1 Thessalonians 2:11-12. *Thought of the members of the Christian community as his children and other family members*: e.g., Galatians 6:10.
2. For example, 1 Thessalonians 5:25; 2 Thessalonians 3:13. The Greek *adelphoi*, which is often rendered "brothers" in the Bible, is also translated "brothers and sisters." Paul uses the word dozens of times.
3. Galatians 4:19; 1 Thessalonians 2:7.
4. Ephesians 2:14-22.
5. James W. Thompson, *Moral Formation according to Paul: The Context and Coherence of Pauline Ethics* (Baker Academic, 2011), 56.

6. J. Paul Sampley, *Walking in Love: Moral Progress and Spiritual Growth with the Apostle Paul* (Fortress Press, 2016), xiii.
7. Thompson, *Moral Formation*, 64.
8. Thompson, *Moral Formation*, 64: "1 Thessalonians is largely composed of repetition of the earlier catechesis for new converts (cf. 2:12). Thus Paul's moral instructions are neither arbitrary nor ad hoc responses to crises, but a concrete and coherent vision of the life that is worthy of the gospel."
9. Reidar Aasgaard, *"My Beloved Brothers and Sisters!": Christian Siblingship in Paul* (T&T Clark, 2004), 54.
10. Robert Mulholland Jr. defines *spiritual formation* as "a process of being formed in the image of Christ for the sake of others." M. Robert Mulholland Jr., *Invitation to a Journey: A Road Map for Spiritual Formation*, expanded by Ruth Haley Barton (IVP Books, 2016), 16. First Thessalonians 4:12 states the result of practicing these commands is that the church will walk worthily before outsiders. James Thompson claims that Paul was not primarily concerned with moral issues "in a narrow sense" but rather with Christian formation in general. Thompson, *Moral Formation*, 60.
11. In her work on silence, which we will consider in greater depth, Maggie Ross says that silence is to be pursued holographically rather than linearly. The principle applies here as well. Maggie Ross, *Silence: A User's Guide*, vol. 1, *Process* (Cascade Books, 2014), 1.

3 | LOVE DEEPLY

1. Aasgaard states that *adelphoi* can mean "siblings"; thus, "sibling love" is an appropriate, more gender-inclusive rendering of *philadelphia*. Reidar Aasgaard, *"My Beloved Brothers and Sisters!": Christian Siblingship in Paul* (T&T Clark, 2004), 38.
2. Aasgaard, *"My Beloved Brothers and Sisters!"*, 165–66.
3. Chris E. W. Green, personal communication, October 2023.
4. James W. Thompson, *Moral Formation according to Paul: The Context and Coherence of Pauline Ethics* (Baker Academic, 2011), 81.
5. Plutarch, "On Brotherly Love," *Moralia*, trans. William Clark Helmbold, Loeb Classical Library 337, vol. 6 (Harvard University Press, 1939), 249.
6. Aasgaard, *"My Beloved Brothers and Sisters!"*, 106.
7. Aasgaard, *"My Beloved Brothers and Sisters!"*, 157.
8. Aasgaard, *"My Beloved Brothers and Sisters!"*, 3.
9. Aasgaard, *"My Beloved Brothers and Sisters!"*, 151.
10. Nijay K. Gupta, *1 and 2 Thessalonians*, Zondervan Critical Introductions to the New Testament (Zondervan Academic, 2019), 104.
11. Aasgaard, *"My Beloved Brothers and Sisters!"*, 160–61.

Notes

4 | LIVE QUIETLY

1. Marilynne Robinson, *Gilead* (Macmillan, 2005), 20.
2. Augustine Holmes, *A Life Pleasing to God: The Spirituality of the Rules of St Basil* (Cistercian, 2000), 16. Emphasis mine.
3. Leon Morris, *The First and Second Epistles to the Thessalonians*, rev. ed., The New International Commentary on the New Testament (Eerdmans, 1991), 131.
4. Reidar Aasgaard, *"My Beloved Brothers and Sisters!": Christian Siblingship in Paul* (T&T Clark, 2004), 163.
5. St Nikodimos of the Holy Mountain and St Makarios of Corinth, comps., *The Philokalia: The Complete Text*, vol. 1, trans. and ed. G. E. H. Palmer, Philip Sherrard, and Kallistos Ware (Faber and Faber, 1983), 33.
6. Henri Nouwen writes, "A word with power is a word that comes out of silence." Henri J. M. Nouwen, *The Way of the Heart* (Ballantine Books, 1983), 40.
7. Maggie Ross, *Silence: A User's Guide*, vol. 1, *Process* (Cascade Books, 2014), 72.
8. Jamie Kreiner, *The Wandering Mind: What Medieval Monks Tell Us about Distraction* (Liveright, 2023), 167. See Kevin Roose, *Futureproof: 9 Rules for Humans in the Age of Automation* (Random House, 2021), e.g., 168, 172–75.
9. Quoted in Kreiner, *Wandering Mind*, 37.
10. Benedicta Ward, trans., *The Sayings of the Desert Fathers: The Alphabetical Collection*, rev. ed. (Cistercian, 1984), 122.
11. Kreiner, *Wandering Mind*, 33.
12. Regarding the world, Kreiner comments, "'The world' was really just a monastic euphemism for the physical and mental distractions that pulled a person away from God, and so—as one monk put it to another in the seventh century—it was the *tropos* that made a monk, not the *topos*. It was *how* rather than *where* a monk lived that mattered." Kreiner, *Wandering Mind*, 196.
13. Nouwen, *Way of the Heart*, 17.
14. Blaise Pascal, *Pascal's Pensées*, trans. W. F. Trotter (E. P. Dutton, 1958), 39.
15. Ruth Haley Barton, *Invitation to Solitude and Silence: Experiencing God's Transforming Presence*, 2nd ed. (IVP Books, 2010), 31.
16. Ward, *Sayings of the Desert Fathers*, 81.
17. Nouwen, *Way of the Heart*, 37.
18. Ross, *Silence*, vol. 1, 33.
19. Quoted in Maggie Ross, *Silence: A User's Guide*, vol. 2, *Application* (Cascade Books, 2018), 1.
20. Ross, *Silence*, vol. 1, 164.

21. Ross, *Silence*, vol. 1, 13.
22. Ross, *Silence*, vol. 1, 11.
23. Nouwen, *Way of the Heart*, 42.
24. Nouwen, *Way of the Heart*, 53.
25. St. Basil the Great, *The Monastic Rule of St Basil the Great*, trans. Anna Skoubourdis and Monaxi Agapi (Virgin Mary of Australia and Oceania, 2020), 14–15.
26. An endnote hardly seems like enough acknowledgment to confess that this book was written to the audiological backdrop of the War on Drugs.
27. St. John of the Ladder, *The Ladder of Divine Ascent*, trans. Archimandrite Lazarus Moore (independently published, 2019), 76.
28. Ward, *Sayings of the Desert Fathers*, 139.
29. Kreiner, *Wandering Mind*, 14.
30. Kreiner, *Wandering Mind*, 15.
31. Quoted in Kreiner, *Wandering Mind*, 7.
32. Ross, *Silence*, vol. 1, 131.
33. Kreiner, *Wandering Mind*, 23.
34. Kreiner, *Wandering Mind*, 23.
35. Kreiner, *Wandering Mind*, 8.
36. Kreiner, *Wandering Mind*, 196.
37. Evagrios the Solitary teaches, "If you have friends, avoid constant meetings with them. For if you meet only on rare occasions, you will be of more help to them. And if you find that harm comes through meeting them, do not see them at all. The friends that you do have should be of benefit to you and contribute to your way of life. . . . Do not pass your time with people engaged in worldly affairs or share their table, in case they involve you in their illusions and draw you away from the science of stillness. . . . Do not have relationships with too many people, lest your intellect becomes distracted and so disturbs the way of stillness." Nikodimos and Makarios, *Philokalia*, 34–35.
38. David Hester writes, "These few simple words, known as the Jesus Prayer, are of great importance to the Christian East—so much so that they are often called the summation of all Orthodox spirituality." David Hester, *The Jesus Prayer: A Gift from the Fathers* (Conciliar Press, 2001), 5.
39. Let the reader use wisdom and consult his or her physician. For reference (not for prescription), Evagrios the Solitary writes, "Fast before the Lord according to your strength, for to do this will purge you of your iniquities and sins; it exalts the soul, sanctifies the mind, drives away the demons, and prepares you for God's presence. Having already eaten once, try not to eat a second time the same day, in case you become extravagant and disturb your

mind." In principle, you can see how the monks viewed food as part of their attempt at quiet living. Nikodimos and Makarios, *Philokalia*, 36.

40. M. Robert Mulholland Jr., *Invitation to a Journey: A Road Map for Spiritual Formation*, expanded by Ruth Haley Barton (IVP Books, 2016).

5 | MIND YOUR OWN AFFAIRS

1. Leon Morris, *The First and Second Epistles to the Thessalonians*, rev. ed., The New International Commentary on the New Testament (Eerdmans, 1991), 131.
2. Quoted in Justin Tosi and Brandon Warmke, *Why It's OK to Mind Your Own Business* (Routledge, 2024), 37.
3. John 21:20-23.
4. Matthew 20:1-16.
5. Henri J. M. Nouwen, with Michael J. Christensen and Rebecca J. Laird, *Spiritual Formation: Following the Movements of the Spirit* (HarperOne, 2010), 58.
6. Matthew 25:14-30.
7. Matthew 13:12.
8. Matthew 19:16-30.
9. Luke 8:1-3.
10. Genesis 3.
11. Arthur Kurzweil, personal communication, circa 2020.
12. In a chapter about minding your own affairs, you'd think there wouldn't be any social media citations. But here we go. I saw this quote on Facebook about something Andy Squyres said during a concert as quoted by Bliss Spillar IV. Bliss Spillar IV, "Tonight was a good night," Facebook, March 11, 2024, https://www.facebook.com/profile/55701884/search/?q=andy%20squyers.
13. Iain McGilchrist, *Ways of Attending: How Our Divided Brain Constructs the World* (Routledge, 2018), 13.
14. Adin Steinsaltz, *The Thirteen Petalled Rose: A Discourse on the Essence of Jewish Existence and Belief*, rev. ed., trans. Yehuda Hanegbi (Maggid Books, 2010), 56.
15. Tosi and Warmke, *Mind Your Own Business*, 3.
16. Tosi and Warmke, *Mind Your Own Business*, 56.
17. Robert D. Lupton, *Toxic Charity: How Churches and Charities Hurt Those They Help (and How to Reverse It)* (HarperOne, 2012).
18. Tosi and Warmke, *Mind Your Own Business*, 7.
19. Tosi and Warmke, *Mind Your Own Business*, 7.
20. Matthew 21:12-13.

21. Matthew 9:10-13.
22. Dietrich Bonhoeffer, *Life Together: The Classic Exploration of Christian Community*, trans. John W. Doberstein (HarperOne, 2009), 99.
23. Jeannine K. Brown, "Just a Busybody? A Look at the Greco-Roman Topos of Meddling for Defining ἀλλοτριεπίσκοπος in 1 Peter 4:15," *Journal of Biblical Literature* 125, no. 3 (2006): 552.
24. Tosi and Warmke, *Mind Your Own Business*, 38.
25. Benedicta Ward, trans., *The Sayings of the Desert Fathers: The Alphabetical Collection*, rev. ed. (Cistercian, 1984), 142.
26. Plutarch, *Moralia*, trans. William Clark Helmbold, Loeb Classical Library 337, vol. 6 (Harvard University Press, 1939), 477.
27. Quoted in Tosi and Warmke, *Mind Your Own Business*, 57.
28. Tosi and Warmke, *Mind Your Own Business*, 23.
29. Plutarch, *Moralia*, vol. 6, 513.
30. Plutarch, *Moralia*, vol. 6, 475.

6 | WORK WITH YOUR HANDS

1. Chris E. W. Green, host, *Speakeasy Theology*, podcast, "Falling into the Mind of Christ: A Conversation with Martin Shaw," June 12, 2024, https://cewgreen.substack.com/p/falling-into-the-mind-of-christ.
2. Miroslav Volf, *Work in the Spirit: Toward a Theology of Work* (Wipf and Stock, 2001), 34.
3. Andy Crouch, *Culture Making: Recovering Our Creative Calling*, expanded ed. (InterVarsity Press, 2023), 75.
4. John Paul II, *Laborem Exercens* [On Human Work], encyclical letter, The Holy See, September 14, 1981, https://www.vatican.va/content/john-paul-ii/en/encyclicals/documents/hf_jp-ii_enc_14091981_laborem-exercens.pdf.
5. "The Protoevangelium of James," New Advent, accessed April 8, 2025, https://www.newadvent.org/fathers/0847.htm.
6. Nijay K. Gupta, *1 and 2 Thessalonians*, Zondervan Critical Introductions to the New Testament (Zondervan Academic, 2019), 132–33.
7. Gupta, *1 and 2 Thessalonians*, 134.
8. Andrew Dinan, "Manual Labor in the Life and Thought of St. Basil the Great," *Logos: A Journal of Catholic Thought and Culture* 12, no. 4 (2009): 139.
9. Gupta, *1 and 2 Thessalonians*, 132.
10. *Adamah* is Hebrew for "ground" or "earth."
11. Volf, *Work in the Spirit*, 127.
12. Genesis 2:5.
13. Genesis 3:23.
14. Genesis 1:28.

Notes

15. Jordan Raynor, *The Sacredness of Secular Work: 4 Ways Your Job Matters for Eternity (Even When You're Not Sharing the Gospel)* (Waterbrook, 2024), 10.
16. Makoto Fujimura, *Art and Faith: A Theology of Making* (Yale University Press, 2020), 11.
17. Fujimura, *Art and Faith*, 64.
18. Charles H. Spurgeon, "All for Jesus!," Sermon 1205, November 29, 1874, Spurgeon Gems, https://www.spurgeongems.org/sermon/chs1205.pdf.
19. Dorothy L. Sayers, "Why Work?," in *Letters to a Diminished Church: Passionate Arguments for the Relevance of Christian Doctrine* (W Publishing Group, 2004), 131–32.
20. Sayers, "Why Work?," 131.
21. Raynor, *Sacredness of Secular Work*, ix.
22. Quoted in Sayers, "Why Work?," 133.
23. Colossians 3:23-24.
24. Jordan B. Peterson, host, *The Jordan B. Peterson Podcast*, episode 472, "A Call to the Sane—Beauty, Truth, & Purpose with Douglas Murray," August 7, 2024, YouTube, August 15, 2024, https://www.youtube.com/watch?v=Rx68_EfSJsE.
25. Viktor E. Frankl, *Man's Search for Meaning* (Beacon Press, 2006), 66.
26. See Ecclesiastes 2:24.
27. Parker J. Palmer, *Let Your Life Speak: Listening for the Voice of Vocation* (Jossey-Bass, 2000), 21.
28. Volf, *Work in the Spirit*, 106.
29. Quoted in Joanne Jung and Rick Langer, "The Strange Tale of How Nicholas Herman Found Meaning in Life," *The Good Book Blog*, Biola University, October 31, 2022, https://www.biola.edu/blogs/good-book-blog/2022/the-strange-tale-of-how-nicholas-herman-found-meaning-in-life.
30. Brother Lawrence, *The Practice of the Presence of God*, trans. John J. Delaney (Image Books, 1977), 16.
31. Raynor, *Sacredness of Secular Work*, 17.
32. Jeremy Sims, personal communication, fall 2023.
33. Thomas Merton, *No Man Is an Island* (Image Books, 1955), 102.
34. Volf writes, "When God calls people to become children of God, the Spirit gives them callings, talents, and 'enablings' (charisms) so that they can do God's will in the Christian fellowship and in the world in anticipation of God's eschatological new creation. All Christians have several gifts of the Spirit. Since most of these gifts can be exercised only through work, work must be considered a central aspect of Christian living." Volf, *Work in the Spirit*, 124.

35. "Big House," track 5 on Audio Adrenaline, *Don't Censor Me*, ForeFront Records, 1993.
36. I understand that to be "absent from the body [is] to be present with the Lord" (2 Corinthians 5:8, KJV). There is an interim state, which Scripture refers to as "paradise," when we are in the presence of God prior to resurrection and prior to heaven coming to earth.
37. Raynor, *Sacredness of Secular Work*, 49–50. Emphasis mine.
38. N. T. Wright, *Surprised by Hope: Rethinking Heaven, the Resurrection, and the Mission of the Church* (HarperOne, 2008), 208.
39. "It is plausible that the statement in Revelation about the saints resting 'from their labors [*kopōn*], for their deeds (*erga*) follow them' (Rev. 14:13; cf. Eph. 6:8) could be interpreted to imply that earthly work will leave traces on resurrected personalities." Volf, *Work in the Spirit*, 97–98.
40. Wright, *Surprised by Hope*, 147–63.

7 | EXPANDING THE CIRCLE

1. Henri J. M. Nouwen, with Michael J. Christensen and Rebecca J. Laird, *Spiritual Formation: Following the Movements of the Spirit* (HarperOne, 2010), 66.
2. For example, the New International Version and the International Standard Version.
3. Chris E. W. Green, personal communication, fall 2023.
4. Hermann Hesse, *The Journey to the East*, trans. Hilda Rosner (Martino, 2011), 25.
5. Hesse, *Journey to the East*, 48.

NavPress
Bold. Loving. Sensible.

Since 1975, NavPress, a business ministry of The Navigators, has been producing books, ministry resources, and *The Message* Bible to help people to know Christ, make Him known, and help others do the same.®

"God doesn't want us to be shy with his gifts, but bold and loving and sensible."
2 Timothy 1:7, *The Message*

Learn more about NavPress:

Learn more about The Navigators:

Find NavPress on social media:

Facebook · Bluesky · X · Instagram · YouTube · TikTok · LinkedIn

CP2044

ALSO BY TOMMY BROWN

The Ache for Meaning: How the Temptations of Christ Reveal Who We Are and What We're Seeking